From Your Friends At **The MAILBOX®**

JANUARY

A MONTH OF IDEAS AT YOUR FINGERTIPS!

PRESCHOOL– KINDERGARTEN

WRITTEN BY

Barbara Backer, Ada Hanley Goren, Lucia Kemp Henry, Angie Kutzer, Suzanne Moore, Janna Omwake, Pamela Kay Priest, Mackie Rhodes, Ann C. Saunders, Dayle Timmons

EDITED BY

Lynn Bemer Coble, Ada Hanley Goren, Carol Rawleigh, Mackie Rhodes, Jennifer Rudisill, Karen P. Shelton, Gina Sutphin

ILLUSTRATED BY

Marilynn G. Barr, Jennifer T. Bennett, Cathy Spangler Bruce, Pam Crane, Teresa Davidson, Clevell Harris, Lucia Kemp Henry, Susan Hodnett, Sheila Krill, Rebecca Saunders, Donna K. Teal

TYPESET BY

David Jarrell, Lynette Maxwell

COVER DESIGNED BY

Jennifer T. Bennett

©1996 by THE EDUCATION CENTER, INC.

All rights reserved.

ISBN# 1-56234-139-1

Manufactured in the United States

10 9 8 7 6 5 4 3

TABLE OF CONTENTS

January Calendar **3**
Highlight special days in the month of January.

"Classroom News" Newsletter **5**
Keep parents up-to-date with this reproducible newsletter.

Celebrate A New Year! **6**
Welcome the new year with these fresh and festive ideas!

It's Snowing! **16**
Explore the wonders of the white delight with this cool unit!

Smitten With Mittens **26**
Warm up to a handful of cross-curricular activities involving
marvelous mittens.

Chillin' Out With Polar Bears **36**
Meet our arctic pals in this science-oriented exploration.

**Eggs, Oatmeal, Cinnamon Bun—
Breakfast Is A Lot Of Fun!** **46**
Good morning! How about a healthy serving of breakfast ideas?

**Hand In Hand:
A Celebration Of Martin Luther King's Birthday** **56**
Share Dr. King's dream with these activities emphasizing harmony
and friendship.

Calendar Explorations **61**
Make a date with your students to learn all about the calendar!

Character Lessons From Fairy-Tale Characters **66**
Explore values and virtues with the Three Little Pigs and
their pals.

Our Phenomenal Prehistoric Pals **76**
You'll dig these "dino-mite" dinosaur lessons!

Calling All Community Helpers! **86**
Doctor, carpenter, truck driver, too—
Lots of hardworking ideas for you!

January Calendar

4—Birthdate of Louis Braille

At the age of 20, the ingenious Louis Braille—blinded from the age of three—published a touch system of reading and writing for the visually impaired. The Braille system uses raised, coded dots punched on thick paper to represent letters, signs, and numbers. Give youngsters firsthand experience with some Braille-like print with this activity. Have each child use a white crayon or white chalk to draw a simple shape, design, or picture on a dark sheet of construction paper. Then have him place his paper on a folded towel and use a blunt-pointed pencil to punch holes along the outline of his figure. Encourage each student—with his eyes closed—to feel the resulting raised outline on the back of a classmate's paper. Can he guess what the raised outline represents? After making their guesses, invite the students to open their eyes and look at the outlines to see if they guessed correctly.

8—National Joygerm Day

What is a *joygerm?* It's a germ that spreads a highly contagious disease that destroys the grumps and "down in the dumps." What are the symptoms of the joygerm disease? Lots of joy, love, and laughter! Take some time today to diagnose whether or not your students are infected with joygerms. To make a joygerm, simply hot-glue two wiggle eyes to a large pom-pom. At circle time, pass the joygerm from child to child. As each student receives the joygerm, invite him to share some joy with the class—a happy thought, a silly word, a funny face, a giggle, or any other joyful noise or gesture. A word of caution! Proceed with this activity *only* if you are prepared to let the disease run its course—it's highly contagious and incurable!

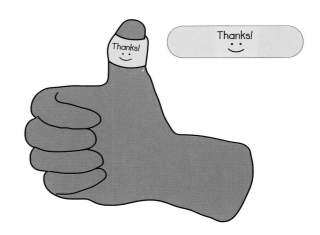

11—International Thank-You Day

It's thumbs-up for thanks today! Have students commemorate this special day of gratitude with these unique reminders to thank "thumb-body" for a kindness. For each student, label a Band-Aid® with the word "Thanks!" and a smiley face. During some part of the day—such as playtime or end-of-the-day activities—wrap a Band-Aid® around each child's thumb. Then, as kindnesses are extended to one another during this period, encourage students to give the thumbs-up sign to express their gratitude.

13—Poetry Break

Have you had your break today? Poetry break, that is? If not, take time on this day to enlighten your little ones with a brief poetry reading. Obtain a copy of an anthology of poems suitable for young children—such as *Poems For The Very Young* selected by Michael Rosen (Kingfisher Books). Then, during storytime or rest time, read aloud one or more selected poems to youngsters. Or read a different poem at several different times throughout the day, signaling each poetry break with the sound of a bell or kitchen timer. It's break time—pick a poem!

21—National Hugging Day™

Invite youngsters to play a special train game today—The Hugga-Chugga-Lugga! Have each student find his own space in a designated area of the classroom. Ask a volunteer to begin the game by chugging up to another child, then giving that child a hug while saying, "Hugga-chugga-lugga." Afterward have the two children position themselves in train-fashion, with the hugged child in front and the other child's hands resting on his shoulders. Then ask the train-leader to approach and hug another child while repeating the phrase. Have that child become the new train-leader. Continue the game in this manner until every student has received a hug and become connected to the train. Then have the Hugga-Chugga-Lugga make several rounds through the classroom. After signaling the train to stop, invite each student to give himself a hug.

24—Discovery Of Gold In California

This momentous event triggered the Gold Rush of 1848—when thousands of people made their way to California looking for their fortunes in gold. Urge students to do a little gold-seeking of their own with this activity. Paint a small rock with gold spray-paint (or cover the rock with gold-foil paper). Place 3–5 small, foil pie plates upside down on a table. While the students are watching, put the gold rock under one of the pie plates. Then randomly slide the pie plates around on the table so that each one is positioned in a location other than its initial position. Have a student volunteer pick the pie plate under which he thinks the gold is hidden. Encourage him to continue guessing until he finds the gold. Then invite him to exchange the gold for a small toy, sticker, or treat. Put the gold under another pie plate; then continue play with another volunteer, proceeding in this manner until every child has had the opportunity to play.

Last Friday In January—Backwards Day

It's Backwards Day—a day when it's acceptable, and even encouraged, to do things backwards! So encourage your little ones to wear their clothes backwards, to say their names backwards, to walk in line backwards, to read a book backwards, and to clean up the room backwards. During outdoor activities, challenge youngsters to perform some exercises—such as running, jumping, crawling, marching, and tiptoeing—backwards. Finally end the day by inviting each child to walk out the door backwards as he leaves.

29—National Puzzle Day

Today pack a punch with puzzles—those often overlooked, underrated sources of overall skill development for youngsters! Gather a large assortment of wooden puzzles, jigsaw puzzles, form-matching games and toys, and other assembly games. Throughout the day—during center activities, free-play choice, quiet time, and any other brief blocks of available time—invite individuals, student pairs, and small groups of students to select activities from the assortment. While little ones enjoy the pleasure of puzzle-play opportunities, you'll be pleased with the productivity of their play!

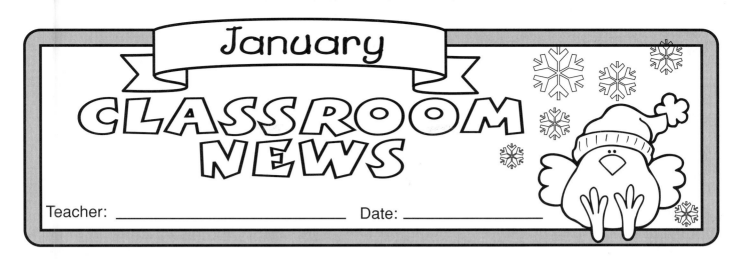

January
CLASSROOM NEWS

Teacher: _____ Date: _____

A Peek At The Week

Looking Ahead

Reminders

Help Wanted

Special Thanks

CELEBRATE A NEW YEAR!

Start the new year off right by celebrating an oh-so-happy holiday! Focus on new beginnings and holiday traditions around the world with the activities in this cross-curricular unit.

ideas contributed by Lucia Kemp Henry

HAPPY BIRTHDAY, NEW YEAR!

Help youngsters understand the concept of a new year with a surprise birthday party! Prepare and frost a sheet cake the day before you plan to begin your New Year's unit. Use tube icing to write "Happy Birthday, [1997]!" on the cake. Then, for each child, cut a sheet of 9" x 12" construction paper as shown. Use a die-cutter to prepare enough numeral cutouts so that each child will have the numerals needed to form the new year's number.

When the children arrive at school, tell them that they will celebrate a special birthday today. Show youngsters a January calendar and point out the first day of the month. Explain that—in the United States—the first day of January is considered the first day of a new year. Show the children the year printed on a calendar or write the numerals representing the new year on the chalkboard. Then invite children to welcome the new year with a birthday celebration.

Demonstrate how to overlap the top two corners of each sheet of construction paper to form a cone-shaped party hat. Staple each child's hat together. Then have each child glue the numerals that represent the new year onto her party hat. If desired, staple a few strips of crinkled gift-wrap stuffing to the point of each hat for a festive flair.

Once youngsters are wearing their hats, teach them this version of "Happy Birthday To You." Then serve each child a slice of cake.

Happy birthday, New Year!
Happy birthday, New Year!
Happy birthday, [1997]!
Happy birthday, New Year!

NEW YEAR...NEW START

Now that youngsters have ushered in the new year in style, give them some background about the holiday. The idea of celebrating a new year has been around since ancient times—practiced by civilizations all over the world. At different times in history and in different cultures, the start of a new year has been celebrated in spring, fall, and winter. But no matter what the calendar date, most ancient and modern celebrations were based on the idea of bringing good luck and prosperity for the coming year.

Ask your youngsters what they know about New Year's celebrations. Do their families have any specific traditions? List their responses on a large sheet of chart paper under the heading "Happy New Year!" Keep the chart paper on display throughout your New Year's unit. Add to the chart as children learn more about various traditions and celebrations.

A NEW SONG

Teach your youngsters this joyous song as a reminder of New Year's traditions and concepts. If desired, accompany the singing of this song with the playing of some student-made noisemakers (from "New Year Noisemakers").

It's A Brand-New Year!
(sung to the tune of "You're A Grand Old Flag")

It's a brand-new year,
So let's give a big cheer!
Blow the horn; beat the drum loud and clear.
Oh, the year's brand-new.
With new things to do.
New things we will learn all the year!

It's a brand-new year,
So let's give a big cheer!
Good-bye, Old Year; the New Year is here.
Should auld acquaintance be forgot—
Say hello to a brand-new year!

NEW YEAR NOISEMAKERS

The modern New Year's Day custom of making celebratory noises with bells, horns, firecrackers, drums, and joyous cheers has its roots in very old traditions. People long ago believed that loud noises would frighten bad luck away from the new year. Ask your youngsters if they have any noisy New Year's Day traditions such as banging pots and pans or blowing noisemakers.

Have your youngsters make their own noisemakers. In advance, collect a class supply of empty potato-chip cans (with a plastic lid for each one). For each child, cut a piece of construction paper that fits around a potato-chip can. Have each child decorate her paper as desired, then glue it around her can. Then set out a variety of fillers for the cans: pennies, dried beans, aquarium gravel, popcorn kernels, and rice. Have each child place a handful of a filler—or a combination of fillers—inside her can. Help her secure the plastic lid on her can; then invite her to shake it up! Use the noisemakers to accompany the song "It's A Brand-New Year!" or during a classroom celebration (see "A New Year's Open House" on page 11).

GREAT GREETINGS

Explain to youngsters that New Year's celebrations take place all over the world. Encourage youngsters to learn how to say, "Happy New Year" in some other languages such as:

Feliz Año Nuevo	Spanish
Hauoli Makahiki Hou	Hawaiian
Bonne Année	French
Gung-Hey-Fat-Choy	Chinese

If the parents or grandparents of any of your students speak another language, ask them to share how to say, "Happy New Year" in that language. Then invite little ones to create cards with New Year's greetings. For each child, duplicate the pattern on page 12 on construction paper. Invite each child to color the front of her card and add touches of glitter, if desired. Then write each child's choice of New Year's greeting on the back of her card. For older children, print a variety of New Year's greetings—in English or foreign languages—on the chalkboard; then encourage each child to copy the greeting of her choice onto her card.

GOOD-LUCK ENVELOPES

Many cultures practice the tradition of wishing one another good luck in the new year. In China, children receive good-luck gifts of money in red envelopes. Invite little ones to make red envelopes containing good-luck wishes for a friend.

For each child, duplicate the envelope and note patterns on page 13 on red construction paper. Have each child cut out the note and envelope along the bold lines. Instruct him to fold the envelope along the thin lines. Then have him sign his name on the note. Help him place the note inside the folded envelope and seal it shut using a gold sticker. Invite each child to give his good-luck note to a friend or a family member.

As a variation, prepare a red note and envelope as directed for each child. Put several gold foil–covered chocolate coins inside each envelope; then seal each one with a gold sticker or gold sealing wax. Present these good-luck gifts to your students at a classroom New Year's celebration (see "A New Year's Open House" on page 11).

NEW YEAR PLANS BOOKLET

The modern idea of making New Year's resolutions reflects the ancient tradition of getting a fresh start for the new year. Youngsters may not fully comprehend the meaning of New Year's resolutions, but they will be able to understand the idea of planning things to do. Introduce the idea by discussing how people make plans for the future. Ask if any of your youngsters have helped a parent plan for a birthday party or a family vacation. After a discussion about planning, explain that some people make plans for the new year—such as ways to improve themselves, new things to learn, or places to visit.

Ask each youngster to make some plans for the new year by completing the reproducible booklet on pages 14 and 15. In advance, duplicate the booklet pages and cutouts on white construction paper for each child. Make a few photocopies of each child's school picture for use in the booklets. Gather a supply of old magazines or catalogs. Then assist each youngster in cutting apart the patterns along the bold lines. Stack the six booklet pages in order and staple them along the left edge. Save the door and book cutouts for later use. Have each youngster follow the directions below to complete her booklet. Encourage each youngster to take her booklet home to share with her family.

Page 1: Write your name on the line. Write the numerals that represent the new year in the open space.

Page 2: Glue a photocopy of your school picture inside the frame, or draw and color a self-portrait in the frame.

Page 3: Glue or draw a picture of a place you'd like to visit.

Page 4: Choose a classmate you'd like to get to know better in the coming year. Glue a photocopy of that classmate's picture on the page. Glue the door cutout to the side of the page where indicated, so it covers the photocopied picture.

Page 5: Glue or draw a picture of something you want to do to help someone.

Page 6: Glue or draw a picture of something you'd like to learn how to do. Glue the book cutout to the side of the page where indicated, so it covers the picture. Fill in the blank.

My
Happy
New Year
Plans

1997

by Zachary

1

Here are my plans
for the year that's new.
There are lots of things
that I want to do!

2

AROUND THE WORLD AT NEW YEAR'S

Introduce little ones to some New Year's traditions from other countries and other cultures. Use the ideas on these two pages to prepare a New Year's menu, clean up the classroom, and hold a New Year's Open House as a culmination to your multicultural study.

A SWEET YEAR

Rosh Hashanah, the Jewish New Year, falls sometime in September or October. Rosh Hashanah is a religious holiday and a time when people think about what they have done in the past year and try to right any wrongs they may have committed. Sweet foods are eaten on Rosh Hashanah to express the wish for a sweet year.

Invite your youngsters to enjoy a popular Rosh Hashanah treat. Have your little ones help you slice several apples. Serve each child a few apple slices, along with some honey in a paper cup.

SURPRISE!

In Greece, a special cake called *vassilopita*—or St. Basil's cake—is prepared on New Year's Day. The cake is baked with a lucky coin hidden inside. It is believed that the person who finds the coin in her slice of cake will have good luck in the coming year.

Adapt this tradition by preparing a batch of Surprise Muffins. Purchase a box of blueberry muffin mix that contains a can of blueberries. Follow the directions on the box to make the batter without stirring in the blueberries. Fill each paper-lined cup in a muffin tin half-full of batter. Drop a scant teaspoonful of the canned blueberries in the center of each cup of batter. Then add enough batter to fill each cup two-thirds full. Bake the muffins as directed on the box. Your youngsters will enjoy biting into their muffins to find the sweet surprise inside!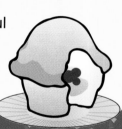

GOOD-LUCK COOKIES

On New Year's Day in Austria, children are given gifts of small toy pigs. These pigs are often made of wood or clay and usually come with a good-luck coin or a four-leaf clover in their mouths. Some pigs are made of edible almond paste called *marzipan*.

Invite youngsters to help you prepare a batch of pig-shaped cookies to follow the Austrian custom. Knead red food coloring into a roll of refrigerator sugar-cookie dough to tint the dough pink. Then roll the dough onto a floured surface. Encourage each child to use a pig-shaped cookie cutter to cut a cookie from the dough. Lay each child's cookie on a cookie sheet covered with waxed paper. Have each child place a green, clover-shaped cake decoration onto his cookie, near the mouth of the pig. Bake the cookies as directed on the package. After the cookies have cooled, serve them to your lucky youngsters!

CLEANING HOUSE

An important part of the Japanese New Year's holiday is a ceremonial housecleaning. Extend this idea to your classroom by asking youngsters to help you give your classroom a thorough cleaning. Have little ones help you clean desks and cubbies and straighten up centers. Give the room a face-lift with new bulletin-board decorations, desktags, or cubby labels. Now your room is clean and ready for visitors (see "A New Year's Open House").

EVERYONE LOVES A PARADE!

Follow a Chinese New Year's custom by planning a dragon parade! In China and in many Chinese-American communities, dancers dressed in dragon costumes parade through the streets and visit places of business to scare away evil spirits and bring good luck for the coming year.

Invite your little ones to create dragon puppets to hold in their own New Year's parade. Provide a class supply of paper lunch bags, as well as collage materials—such as construction paper, cotton balls, wrapping paper, tissue paper, crepe-paper streamers, wiggle eyes, and sequins. Equip the children with scissors and glue, and let their imaginations go to work! After the puppets are completed, encourage each child to slip a hand inside her puppet and introduce it to the class. Then set the puppets aside until you are ready to hold your parade. (You might want to make the parade part of the festivities for "A New Year's Open House.")

I hope 1997 is the best year ever!
Mrs. Cates

I hope school is fun for Miss Stone's Class!
Mr. Davis

A NEW YEAR'S OPEN HOUSE

After talking about customs from all over the world, culminate your unit with a tradition from colonial America—an Open House! Many of our ancestors opened their homes and provided a feast for visitors on New Year's Day. In that same spirit, open your classroom for a visit from parents. Send home a student-made invitation with each child a few days before your event. Invite youngsters to help you prepare a paper banner that reads "New Year's Wishes." Then prepare the treats on page 10 for Open House snacks. On the day of your Open House, lay the banner across a long table. When visitors arrive, invite them to use markers to write wishes for the new year on the banner. If desired, invite parents to watch as their children participate in a parade holding the dragon puppets they created in "Everyone Loves A Parade!"

You might also want to include some noisy singing (see the activities on page 7) or good-luck wishes (see the activities on page 8) as part of the festivities. Whatever you include, have a Happy New Year!

New Year's Card Pattern

Use with "Great Greetings" on page 8.

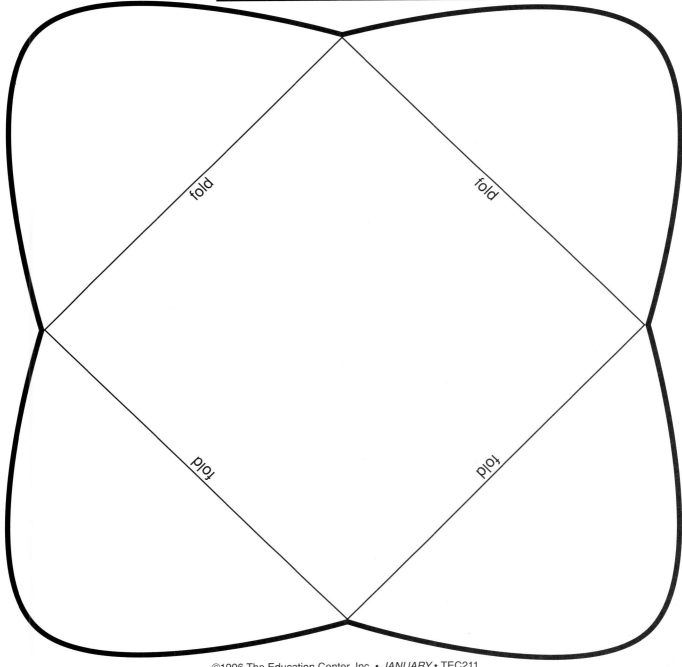

Good Luck
in the
New Year!

fold

fold

fold

fold

My Happy New Year Plans

by _____

1

Here's a place I want to **go...**

3

Here are my plans for the year that's new. There are lots of things that I want to do!

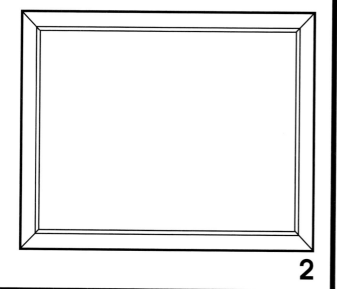

2

Here's someone I'd like to **know...**

Glue door pattern here.

4

I'd like to try
to **help** someone...

5

I'd like to **learn**
this thing for fun!

Glue book pattern here.

6

Glue this pattern to page 4 of the booklet.

Glue this pattern to page 6 of the booklet.

All
About

It's Snowing!

Here's an avalanche of snow-related ideas to warm up those cold, wintry days!

ideas contributed by Barbara Backer and Mackie Rhodes

What Is Snow?

Youngsters may not understand the scientific definition of *snow*—"precipitation in the form of small white ice crystals formed from water vapor at a temperature of less than 32°F"—but they do have definite ideas about what snow is! To find out what your students know about snow, divide a sheet of chart paper into three columns. Label each column with the heading "Snow looks," "Snow feels," or "Other Words About Snow." Then encourage youngsters to describe some things about snow. Ask them to decide in which column each of their descriptions fit. Youngsters might say the snow *looks* "white," "pretty," and "shiny," or *feels* "cold," "wet," and "crunchy." They might use words such as "falls," "melts," and "blows" for the last column of the chart. After completing the chart, share some of these snow facts with students.

- All snowflakes have six sides.
- Snowflakes fall in many different sizes and shapes.
- When snow melts, it becomes water.
- Snow helps protect plants and hibernating animals from the winter cold.

Snow looks	Snow feels	Other Words About Snow
white pretty shiny fluffy	cold wet crunchy	falls melts blows

Up Close And Personal

If snow is common in your area, invite little ones to take a close-up, personal view of some snowflakes. To capture snowflakes, place a piece of dark-colored flannel, velvet, or felt fabric outdoors during a snowfall. After catching several flakes of snow on the fabric, bring them indoors and have youngsters examine them with magnifying glasses. Ask students to describe what they observe. "Do all the snowflakes look the same? Are they the same size?" As the snowflakes melt, place the fabric outdoors again to capture more flakes. Continue in this manner, giving every child an opportunity to examine the snowflakes.

If you are not in an area where snow falls readily, provide pictures (an encyclopedia may be a good source) or acrylic or paper models of snowflakes for students to examine and compare.

The Meltdown

After examining individual snowflakes and watching as they disappear (see "Up Close And Personal" on page 16), children may have a basic understanding that snow becomes water as it melts. To reinforce their understanding of the snow-to-water transformation, try this activity. Fill several clear plastic containers with different quantities of snow (or shaved or crushed ice, if snow is not available). Mark the level of the snow in each container with a permanent marker or a strip of tape. Set the containers aside at an indoor location. Every 15 minutes or so, invite students to check the containers to observe what is happening to the snow. Encourage youngsters to discuss the changes they observe as the snow melts. Guide them to understand that when snowflakes melt, they become plain water.

Then mark the level of the melted snow in each container. Have students compare the two lines on each container. Ask them to speculate why the line for the snowflakes is higher than that for the melted snow. Explain that the snowflakes had lots of air between them, causing the snow to take up extra space. The water resulting from the melted snow filled in the space taken up by air between the snowflakes, so there appears to be less water than there was snow. Actually the amount of water and air in the containers remained constant—only the arrangement of space taken up by each was changed!

To further reinforce the concept that air takes up space, give each youngster a zippered plastic bag partially filled with puffed rice cereal. Ask each student to note the amount of cereal in his bag; then have him crush the air out of the cereal by squeezing the bag between his fingers. Does the bag contain the same amount of cereal? Explain that the puffed cereal seemed to take up more space in the bag than the crushed cereal because it was full of air—just as the air between the snowflakes made them appear to take more space than the melted snow. Afterward, invite each child to sprinkle his crushed cereal outdoors for the birds to eat.

Fantasy Flakes

Turn your classroom into a winter wonderland filled with flurrying, student-created fantasy flakes. To make a snowflake, draw a large, broad X on a piece of waxed paper. Then draw a line across the X as shown to make a six-pointed figure. Have a child trace the lines with streams of white glue. Encourage him to add other touches of glue to create his own unique snowflake design. Then invite him to sparingly sprinkle silver glitter over his glue snowflake. Set the snowflakes aside to dry for several days (they are completely dry if they are not limp when picked up). Shake off any excess glitter; then poke a hole in each snowflake. Thread a length of yarn through the hole and tie the ends together. Hang the snowflakes all around the room—from the ceiling, in the windows, or around the bulletin board— to create a winter wonderland for learning and play!

A-Snowin' We Will Go!

If the weather in your climate already resembles a winter wonderland, have youngsters bundle up and head for the snowy outdoors for some creative movement opportunities. While there, encourage students to explore the many ways they can move in the snow—such as running, tiptoeing, falling, sliding, rolling, and using imaginary skis and sleds. Challenge youngsters to become imaginary snowflakes swirling and twirling slowly in the wind—then moving fast and furiously! Or have students pretend to be little snowballs—then big ones—rolling along the ground. Ask them to become like snowpeople, standing very stiff and still. On your cue, "Melt!", have the students pretend to melt to the ground. Vary your commands to signal children to melt very slowly or very fast. During a melt, you might even give the command "Freeze!" so that youngsters must stop their actions before they actually melt to the ground.

If your weather is not conducive to play in the real thing, invite your little ones to imagine a yard full of snow. It may be helpful to describe the imaginary scene to students. Then have them engage in the movement explorations and activities mentioned. With or without real snow, a-snowin' we will go!

On The Target

Here's a target-practice idea that will hit the bull's-eye with your students! Set three different sizes of laundry baskets outdoors. Invite each youngster, in turn, to pack some snow into a snowball; then, from a specified distance, have him throw the snowball into the designated target—the small, medium, or large basket. Or have the child name which basket he would like to throw his snowball into. Afterward separate the students into three groups. Assign each group a basket and ask the members of each group to pack the snow from their assigned basket into one large snowball. After the groups have formed their snowballs, ask them to decide among themselves if, and how, the three snowballs could be combined to make a snowperson. Encourage youngsters to consider one another's suggestions as they attempt to accomplish this task. If the interest of other students wanes as the natural leaders of each group begin to dominate this activity, invite them to pair up to create smaller versions of snowpeople.

So you don't have snow in your area? No problem! Create your own snow substitute suitable for snowball packing and throwing. Simply immerse white facial tissue in a container of cold water. Then have each youngster pack some of the tissue together—squeezing out the excess water—to form a snowball. After a few rounds of target practice, challenge groups of youngsters to attempt to make larger snowballs from the contents of each basket. Can a snowperson be made from this snow substitute? Whether the answer is yes or no, you're sure to score points with this fun experiment.

Snow Angels

Show off your little snow angels with this heavenly display. While students are out romping in the snow, have each one take a moment to lie down and make a snow angel by simultaneously flapping his arms and moving his legs apart and then together. Take a photo of the child as he creates his snow angel. Indoors invite each child to decorate a duplicated construction-paper cutout of the angel pattern on page 22. Have him glue his developed photo onto the cutout; then write his dictated statement about his photo at the bottom of the cutout. Display the completed angels on a bulletin board titled "Angels In The Snow."

If you do not have snow in which youngsters can make angels, invite each child to lie on the floor and imagine he is in snow. Take his photo as he demonstrates the motions to make a snow angel. Then have each youngster embellish an angel cutout (from page 22). Have him glue his photo onto the cutout; then write his dictation describing his photo. Display the angels with the title "How To Make Snow Angels."

Amber

I fly like an angel.

Decorated Drifts

Bring miniature snowdrifts into your classroom for some colorful fun! Shovel some snow into your classroom water table or into plastic tubs or dishpans. Place plastic shovels, scoops, and spoons nearby. Then provide youngsters with wide paintbrushes and several containers of water each tinted with a different shade of food coloring. Encourage students to paint the snow as desired, using the available utensils to uncover fresh snow to be painted. Or have youngsters shape some snow into balls or other figures and paint them. As the colors blend in the snow, engage the children in a discussion about how new colors can be created with different color combinations.

If snow is not readily available, consider using a substitute—such as finely crushed ice—for this activity. The snow substitute may not provide the same results as the real thing, but students will nevertheless enjoy the sensory experiences.

A Warm, Wintry Treat

After playing in the icy, cold snow of winter, youngsters will be ready for a warm, tasty treat—snowman cookies! Give each child a ball of refrigerated sugar-cookie dough. Have him separate his dough into two or three smaller balls; then have him flatten the balls onto a cookie sheet, overlapping them to resemble a snowman. Invite the student to put chocolate chips on his snowman to represent eyes, buttons, and a nose. Then help him position a cherry-half for his snowman's mouth. Bake the cookies according to the package directions. After the cookies have cooled, serve them to students with cups of warm chocolate. Mmmmm! Yummy!

Disappearing Snowman Cookies

Recite this rhyme as youngsters make snowman-cookie figures disappear before your very eyes! To prepare, photocopy page 24 for later use. Then laminate and cut out the snowman cookies on page 23. Attach the hook side of a piece of Velcro® to the back of each cookie cutout; then place the cutouts on a flannelboard. Invite a child to remove a cutout at the appropriate time in the rhyme. Ask the other children to perform the actions to the rhyme.

[Four] cookie snowmen sitting on a tray.	*Hold up four fingers.*
[Four] cookie snowmen, smiling all day.	*Point to smiling mouth.*
Along came a little child, rubbing his tummy.	*Rub tummy.*
One cookie disappeared. Yum, yum, yummy!	*Hold up one finger and lick lips.*

Repeat the rhyme three more times—the first time replacing the underlined numbers with *three,* then with *two,* and finally with *one.* During each verse have a different child remove the cookie cutouts.

Snowpeople Patterns

Give youngsters lots of patterning and sequencing practice with these snowpeople patterns. On white construction paper, duplicate several copies of the snowpeople patterns on page 24. Color the patterns so that each same-sized set is identical. Laminate and then cut out the patterns. To use them, have a child create a pattern with the sets of cutouts. Or invite the child to sequence each set of snowpeople by size: from largest to smallest or smallest to largest.

Memory Freeze

Use this Concentration-style memory game to encourage little ones to "freeze" information in their minds. Make two copies of the game cards on page 25. Color both sets identically. Mount the cards on tagboard; then laminate them for durability and cut them apart.

To play Memory Freeze, spread the cards facedown on a table. Have a player turn over two cards. If the cards match, he may keep them. But if the cards are different, ask all the players to "freeze" the picture on each card and that card's placement in their memories. Then turn the two cards over. As each child in turn reveals the first of his two cards, encourage him to try to recall if—and where—he has seen the match to it. Continue play until all the matches have been found.

Button Up!

Invite students to practice counting skills while using buttons to decorate snowmen. To prepare snowman cards, duplicate ten copies of the largest snowman pattern on page 24 on white construction paper. Color each snowman; then label each one with a different numeral from 0–9. Laminate the patterns for durability. Place the snowman cards in a learning center along with a container of at least 45 buttons. A child places the number of buttons on each snowman that corresponds with its labeled numeral. For an additional challenge, have the student put the snowman cards in numerical sequence.

A Cool Place To Read

Provide youngsters with a cool reading center where they can enjoy some snow-related literature. Fill a small plastic or inflated pool with white cotton balls or packing peanuts to represent snow. Surround the snow-filled pool with sheets of white quilt batting; then place an assortment of books about snow on the batting. Invite students to take turns sitting in the snow as they melt into a good snow story.

The Snowy Day
Written by Ezra Jack Keats
Published by Scholastic Inc.

Snowballs
Written by Lois Ehlert
Published by Harcourt Brace & Company

Amy Loves The Snow
Written by Julia Hoban
Published by Scholastic Inc.

Just A Snowy Day
Written by Mercer Mayer
Published by Western Publishing Company, Inc.

The First Snowfall
Written by Anne & Harlow Rockwell
Published by Macmillan Publishing Company

Snow Is Falling
Written by Franklyn M. Branley
Published by Thomas Y. Crowell Junior Books

Winter Rabbit
Written by Patrick Yee
Published by Scholastic Inc.

Sledding
Written by Elizabeth Winthrop
Published by Scholastic Inc.

Angel Pattern
Use with "Snow Angels" on page 19.

©1996 The Education Center, Inc.

Snowpeople Patterns

Use with "Snowpeople Patterns" on page 20.
Use the largest snowman with "Button Up!" on page 21.

Smitten With Mittens

No matter where you live, January is probably one of the coldest months of the year. Keep your youngsters' hands busy and warm with these marvelous mitten ideas!

ideas contributed by Ada Hanley Goren and Janna Omwake

A Mitten Mixer

Introduce the topic of mittens with a cooperative activity. A few days prior to beginning your mitten unit, gather enough pairs of mittens to have a pair for every two children. Or duplicate the pair-of-mittens pattern on page 32 onto various colors of construction paper; then cut out and decorate pairs to make enough for each child to have one mitten.

As students enter your classroom on the first day of your mittens unit, give each child a mitten—real or paper—to hold. When everyone has arrived, ask each child to find the youngster holding the mate to his mitten. Then explain this fun cooperative activity. Ask each student to sit facing his partner and pretend he is looking into a mirror. Have each child in a pair take a turn as the leader. Ask the leader to perform a series of movements (of his choice) using his mitten—such as placing the mitten on his nose, tapping his head with the mitten, or putting the mitten on his hand and waving. His partner performs the same motions, simulating a mirror image. Continue the activity until each child has had a turn to be the leader a few times.

Why Mittens?

Discuss with youngsters why people wear mittens. Ask them to brainstorm a list of other winter clothing that protects people from the cold. Then try this hands-on experience. In advance, prepare a tray of ice cubes and gather a few pairs of real mittens. Working with a few children at a time, hand each child an ice cube: first in her bare hands, then while she is wearing a pair of mittens. Ask her to describe the difference in the way her hands felt while holding the ice with and without the mittens. After all the children have participated in the ice-cube activity, teach them this song about the purpose of mittens.

Mittens Feel So Nice
(sung to the tune of "Row, Row, Row Your Boat")

Warm, warm, warm and snug—
Mittens feel so nice!
So grab a pair in chilly air
Or in the snow and ice!

Mittens Vs. Gloves

Do your youngsters prefer to wear mittens or gloves? Create a class graph to find out! Prepare a large sheet of bulletin-board paper with the title "Do You Like Mittens Or Gloves?" Write the headings "Mittens" and "Gloves" on the left side of the graph. Distribute a half-sheet of construction paper to each child. Explain that if she prefers to wear gloves, she should trace around each finger and thumb on one hand; then have her cut on her outline to create a glove-shaped cutout. If she prefers to wear mittens, have her trace a mitten shape around her four fingers and thumb; then ask her to cut out that shape. Have each child label her cutout with her name, then affix it to the appropriate row on the graph using rolled masking tape or Sticky-Tac. Together with your youngsters, count the votes on each line to determine the class preference. Use the graph to discuss the concepts of *more* and *fewer*.

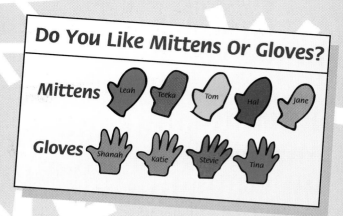

Do You Like Mittens Or Gloves?

Mittens: Leah, Teeka, Tom, Hal, Jane

Gloves: Shanah, Katie, Stevie, Tina

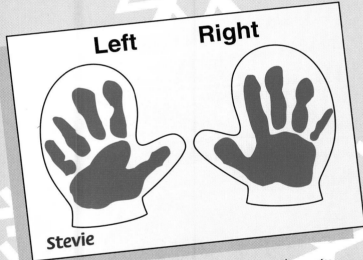

Left   Right

stevie

One For The Left And One For The Right

This handy-dandy activity will help youngsters learn to identify *left* and *right*. Duplicate the pair-of-mittens pattern on page 32 on construction paper for each child. Then prepare a shallow tray of tempera paint with a little dish detergent mixed into it. Working with one or two children at a time, invite each student to press one hand at a time into the paint, then onto the mitten outline that corresponds to that hand (left or right). As each child makes his handprints, remind him which hand is his left and which is his right. Point out the words "Left" and "Right" printed above the mittens. Encourage the children to take the completed papers home and display them on their refrigerators or in their rooms as visual reminders of left and right.

Mitten Munchies

Emphasize the idea of a *pair* when you invite little ones to make mitten-shaped snacks. Cut two mitten-shaped slices of bread for each child. (A mitten-shaped cookie cutter would be helpful for this task.) Ask each child to arrange his two mitten shapes with the thumbs together, to make a mirror-image pair. Then invite him to spread peanut butter or cream cheese on top of each bread shape. Provide decorations for the mittens, such as carrot rounds, thinly sliced celery, raisins, and coconut. Encourage each child to decorate his two mittens identically to create a matching pair. Then invite him to munch those mittens—either one at a time or as a mitten sandwich!

A Favorite Story

No unit on mittens would be complete without a reading of *The Mitten* adapted by Jan Brett (G. P. Putnam's Sons). Share this beautifully illustrated adaptation of an old Ukrainian folktale with your youngsters. Then use the animal patterns on page 33 to create a storytelling set for little ones to use. (Before beginning, you may wish to make some color copies of page 33 for use in other activities. See "Nicki Says" on this page.) After duplicating the patterns on page 34 for later use, mount page 33 on a sheet of tagboard. Cut out the individual animals; then laminate all the pieces for durability. Create a mitten shape by cutting two small sheets of poster board into identical mitten shapes. Staple or glue their edges together, leaving the cuff edge open so that students can insert the animal cutouts. Store the cutouts inside the poster-board mitten; then place the mitten and a copy of the book in your reading center for youngsters to use in retelling the story.

Nicki Says

Use the animal patterns on page 33 to help students practice positional concepts. Prepare the cutouts as directed for the activity described in "A Favorite Story." Then use either a real or a poster-board mitten for this small-group version of Simon Says. Use the name of the boy from the story—Nicki—in place of Simon. Place the cutouts and the mitten on a tabletop. Give a direction to one child in a small group, such as, "Nicki says, 'Put the bear *on* the mitten,' or "Nicki says, 'Make the badger hop *over* the mitten.' " Then have the child follow your direction using the named animal pattern—but only if Nicki says so! Continue until each child in the group has had the opportunity to demonstrate his understanding of several positional words. Then repeat the activity with the remaining groups.

As a variation, make a few color copies of page 33. Prepare multiple sets of the animal cutouts. After working with the children in a small group as described, divide the group into sets of partners. Give each pair of students a set of animal cutouts and a mitten. Have each child, in turn, give directions for his partner to follow using the cutouts and mitten. The children will love trying to trick one another by omitting the phrase "Nicki says."

A Mitten Without Knittin'

After hearing about Baba's fine knitting in *The Mitten* by Jan Brett (see "A Favorite Story" on page 28), your little ones will want to craft their own mittens. While you probably don't want to conduct a knitting lesson in your early-childhood classroom, you can invite youngsters to imitate sewing with this fine-motor activity. In advance, purchase several sheets of plastic canvas from a craft store. Cut each sheet of canvas into seven-inch squares, making one square for each child. Then use one of the mitten patterns from page 32 to make a template from tagboard. Use a permanent marker to trace around the mitten template on each plastic canvas square. Then provide each child with a large, plastic safety needle and various colors of yarn.

Demonstrate how to thread a needle and to stitch yarn in and out of the holes in the canvas. Encourage each youngster to "sew" around the outline of her mitten, then create designs inside the mitten outline with various colors of yarn. As a variation—one that is particularly good for younger preschoolers—let the students "sew" with long pipe cleaners. These are stiffer and easier for little fingers to manipulate. The result will be an interesting, fuzzy texture and some marvelous mittens!

A Class Book Of Mittens

Encourage little ones to use descriptive words with this class book activity. For each child, duplicate the class book page on page 34. Make one additional copy to use as a template for the book's covers. Have each child use either her own real mittens or a pair of paper mittens that she has decorated for the source of her description. Then have each child pose with her mittens as you snap a photo. Ask each child to glue the developed photo to her book page; then ask her to provide three descriptive words or phrases about her mittens for you to write on the blanks. Have her cut around the outline to create a mitten-shaped book page.

Use the extra book page as a template to trace front and back covers on poster board. Cut out the covers; then stack the students' pages between the covers and bind the book with two metal rings at the side. Print the title "Our Mitten Book" on the front cover and place the book in your classroom reading area for children to enjoy.

My mittens are
___ warm ___,
___ fuzzy ___,
and ___ yellow ___.

29

Musical Mitten Matchups

Give little ones a chance to practice visual-discrimination skills with this musical mitten game. Use pairs of real mittens or create pairs of paper mittens following the directions described in "A Mitten Mixer" on page 26. During circle time, place one mitten from each pair on the floor in your circle area. Put the mate from each pair in a box or basket. Then teach youngsters this song to sing as the game is played.

Once students know the song, invite one child at a time to come forward to play the game. Give him one of the mittens from the box or basket. Have the child's classmates sing the song as he searches the mittens on the floor to find the mate to the one he is holding. After he has located the matching mitten, allow him to choose the next child to play the game. Then replace the mittens from the found pair before the next round of play. Continue until all the children have had a turn to find a pair.

Each Mitten Has A Mate

(sung to the tune of "If You're Happy And You Know It")

Each mitten has a mate, has a mate.
Each mitten has a mate, has a mate.
Can [Child's name] find the pair?
[He/She] is looking here and there.
Can [Child's name] find the mate,
  find the mate?

Mitten Magnets

A pair of mitten magnets will provide a handy way for parents to display winter art projects at home *and* give little ones a chance to practice cutting skills with a unique material. In advance, duplicate the pair-of-mittens pattern on page 32 onto tagboard. Cut out the mittens; then use the cutouts as templates to trace a pair of mittens onto a sheet of craft foam for each child. (If you wish to use a smaller supply of craft foam, use a smaller mitten pattern from page 35 to complete this project.)

Have each child cut out his pair of mittens. Encourage him to use craft glue to affix a variety of art materials—such as sequins, scrap pieces of craft foam, cotton balls, rickrack, or ribbon—to his pair of mittens. Use a permanent marker to write "[Child's name]'s" on the left mitten's cuff and "Work" on the right mitten's cuff. After the glue has dried completely, attach a piece of magnetic tape to the back of each mitten. Send each child's attractive artwork home for his parents to display on the family refrigerator!

Missing Mittens

Give youngsters practice with critical thinking when you play a Missing Mittens game. Begin this activity with a reading of the traditional nursery rhyme "The Three Little Kittens." Then have your little ones hunt for some missing mittens, just as the three little kittens did. Invite one child to play the part of a kitten. Have her turn her back to the group as a classmate hides a pair of mittens somewhere in the classroom. Then have the kitten turn around. Have the other children give her clues as to where the mittens are hidden. After the kitten finds the mittens, have her choose the next child to play the role of the kitten. Repeat the activity until each child has had a turn to hunt for missing mittens. When each of your little kittens has found her mittens, celebrate with—what else?—a pie! Serve slices of store-bought cream pie to your youngsters for a "purr-fect" ending to this activity.

Mitten Manipulatives

Mittens make magnificent manipulatives! Duplicate the patterns on page 35 as many times as desired on construction paper, tagboard, or colored cardstock. Cut out the mittens; then laminate all the pieces for durability. Follow the suggestions below or think of some variations of your own for using the mittens to help your students practice a variety of math and language skills.

- Program each of several mittens with a numeral or letter in a series. String a length of yarn between two chairs to resemble a clothesline. Provide clothespins and encourage children to clip the mittens on the line in numerical or alphabetical order.
- Invite youngsters to sort the mittens by color, size, or design.
- Invite youngsters to practice patterning with the mittens.
- Program matching pairs of mittens with rhyming words, upper- and lowercase letters, numerals and sets, matching shapes, or any other basic skill you wish to have your students practice. Ask the children to match the mitten pairs according to the programmed skill.

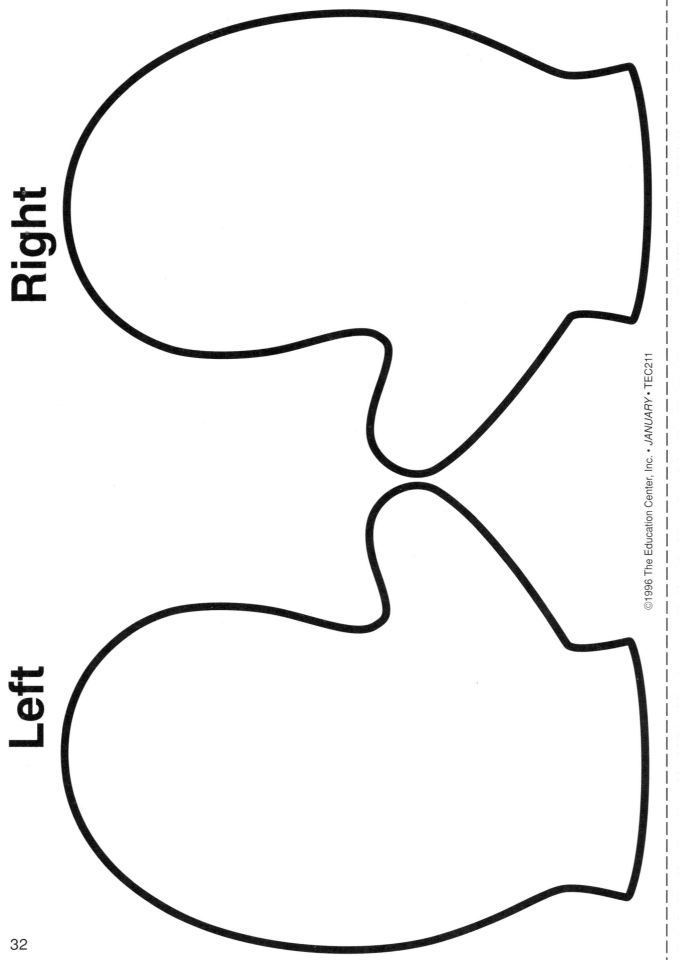

Right

Left

Note To The Teacher: Use with "A Mitten Mixer" on page 26, "One For The Left And One For The Right" on page 27, "A Mitten Without Knittin'" on page 29, and "Mitten Magnets" on page 30.

Chillin' Out With Polar Bears

Fascinate youngsters with the bear facts—and lots of fun, interesting activities—about the amazing polar bear, the white giant of the Arctic!

ideas contributed by Lucia Kemp Henry and Mackie Rhodes

The "Bear" Facts

Little ones will "bear-ly" realize they're learning important information when you share these amazing facts about the beautiful, unique polar bear.

- Polar bears live near the North Pole—a cold region where snowstorms are frequent and icebergs float in the freezing seas.
- Polar bears are *nomadic*—they wander from place to place, traveling on drifting ice and swimming the cold seas of the north.
- Polar bears have thick white fur which protects them from the cold and also *camouflages*—or hides—them while they hunt for food.
- Polar bears are excellent hunters. They use their keen sense of smell to locate food—sometimes miles away! They mostly hunt and eat seals.
- Polar bears have furry feet and sharp claws which help them travel over ice and snow.
- A baby polar bear is so small it can fit into your hand. But a full-grown polar bear may be as long as 11 feet and weigh as much as 1,000 pounds!
- Fortunately, polar bears adapt well to zoo life, so many people have the opportunity to see them without traveling to the North Pole!

A Giant White Bear

Give youngsters firsthand experience with the actual size of a polar bear with this life-size figure. To make the giant white bear, use an opaque projector to enlarge the smelling bear figure on page 43 to a height of approximately five feet. Trace the bear onto a double-wide length of light blue bulletin-board paper (two identical lengths of paper taped together). Have small groups of students take turns using white tempera paint to sponge-paint the bear. After the paint dries, glue black construction-paper eyes and a nose on the bear's face. Use a black marker to fill in the bear's ears. Then cut out the bear and tape it to a wall with its feet touching the floor.

Invite each youngster to stand beside the giant polar bear to have his picture taken; then have him mount his photo on a half-sheet of construction paper. Encourage each child to write (or dictate) a sentence about himself and the polar bear on his paper. Display the photos on the wall surrounding the bear with the title "This Bear Is Big!"

Where Is That Bear?

Although some students may be acquainted with the polar bear from zoo visits, they most likely are not aware of the location of the bear's natural habitat. Try this activity to help youngsters understand a little about the geography of the polar bear's natural home. Make a reduced copy of one of the polar bears on page 43; then cut out the bear. Explain to students that the polar bear lives in an area called the Arctic. Point out that the Arctic is near the North Pole and is located at the *top* of the earth. Using a globe, help youngsters locate the North Pole. Describe the cold, wintry weather that prevails in that area. Then invite a volunteer to tape the polar bear cutout onto the North Pole region of the globe. If desired, help students locate the Antarctic, or South Pole, at the *bottom* of the globe. Explain that, although the weather conditions in the North and South Pole are similar, polar bears live only in the North Pole regions. Now, where can you find that bear?

Totally White And Out Of Sight!

The polar bear's white fur blends with the snowy landscape to camouflage the bear, enabling it to sneak up on its prey without being seen. To give youngsters an idea about what camouflage means and how it works, do this simple activity. Cut a length of white bulletin-board paper to represent the snowy arctic landscape. Cut five polar bear shapes from the same white paper. Then cut five polar bear shapes each from brown and black construction paper. Randomly place the 15 bear cutouts on the paper. Challenge a child to find and pick up all the bears as quickly as possible. Which bears are more easily found? Which ones are harder to spot? After the child finds the bears, ask him to count them. Did he find all of the bears? Then place a random number of white bears on the paper. Ask the child to find all of the white bears. When he believes he has found all the bears, tell him the number that were placed on the paper; then have him count the bears to see if he found all of them.

For additional practice in visual discrimination and figure-ground perception, have students do similar activities with textured materials. For example, place a colorful variety of cotton balls on a sheet of white batting; then ask a child to find all the white cotton balls. Or place an assortment of fabric squares on a length of patterned fabric—some with designs identical to the background fabric and some with different designs—and have the child find all the squares that match the background fabric.

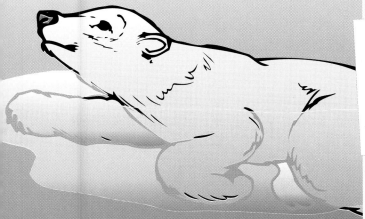

Bear-Footin'

The fur on the soles of a polar bear's feet not only helps the bear keep its footing on ice, but also serves as insulation against the cold. Give youngsters the opportunity to experience how fur can serve as an insulator with this foot-warming activity. Cut two 9" x 12" pieces of faux fur. Have a child remove his shoes and socks. Ask the child to walk barefoot along a tile or vinyl floor, imagining he is walking on arctic ice. Does the floor feel cool? Then wrap a piece of the fur around one of the child's feet and secure it with wide, loose-fitting rubber bands. Again have the child walk around on the floor. Ask him to compare the temperatures of his two feet. Which foot is warmer? Invite the child to wrap the other piece of fur around his other foot, then prowl around like a giant, white, furry-footed bear. After every child has had a turn, serve each a portion of a bear-claw pastry and some ice water.

Just Sniffing Around

Using its keen sense of smell, a polar bear can sniff prey under layers of snow and ice and as far as ten miles away. Youngsters will develop a better understanding of how a polar bear uses its sense of smell when they sniff out their own snacks. In advance, prepare a Jell-O® Jigglers® snack for each child. Put the child's snack on a small paper plate. Put a block or cookie cutter on each of two other paper plates. Completely cover each plate with a paper towel. Then place the three plates at equal distances from one another on a table. Invite a child to imagine she is a polar bear sniffing for her dinner. If desired, have her wear a black, triangular, construction-paper bear nose on her own nose (attached with a piece of rolled tape). Encourage her to sniff each plate without removing its covering; then have her select the plate she believes holds her snack. After each of your little polar bears sniffs out her treat, invite her to enjoy her snack with a cup of juice.

To reinforce how much more keen a polar bear's sniffing ability is than our own, try this experiment. Partially fill a clear plastic dish with water. Drop an aquatic animal-shaped fruit snack into the dish; then place the dish in the freezer. After the water freezes, invite students in turn to sniff the ice. Can they smell the fruit snack embedded in the ice? Place another fruit snack on a plate. Ask youngsters to smell the snack; then have them compare their abilities to smell the food on the plate versus the food frozen in the ice. Explain that a polar bear would be able to smell the food under the ice. Then give each child a few pieces of the fruit snack to reward her sniffing efforts.

A Day In The Life Of A Polar Bear

To summarize some of the daily activities of the great white polar bear, teach youngsters this poem. Duplicate page 44; then cut out and laminate the polar bear pictures on page 43. Attach the hook side of a piece of Velcro® to the back of each picture. Place the appropriate picture on a flannelboard to go along with each verse of the poem. Invite youngsters to perform hand gestures to each of the bear's movements as the poem is recited.

A polar bear walks
On his furry feet so nice.
His claws are short and sharp
So he doesn't slip on ice!

A polar bear swims
In the freezing arctic seas.
He swims and dives and floats
With grace and so much ease.

A polar bear sniffs
The air and ice for seals.
With his nose he finds
Lots of tasty meals.

A polar bear sleeps
Right on the ice, you know.
He curls up in a heap
To stay warm in the snow.

Swimming The Arctic Seas

Swimming is a necessary form of travel for polar bears as they move from place to place searching for food. These white giants often swim from one iceberg to another, paddling with their strong front legs. Invite students to simulate food-seeking, swimming polar bears in an imaginary, ice-filled Arctic sea. To represent icebergs in the sea, arrange four Hula-Hoop® rings on the floor in the shape of a baseball diamond. Randomly place several zippered plastic bags of Gummy Fish® within the area surrounded by the hoops—the sea. Explain that each child will have a turn to imagine he is a polar bear in search of his dinner. Have a different student stand in each of the four rings. Give one child a folded, vinyl rest mat (or a piece of cardboard) and instruct him to lie facedown on it. Then encourage him to use his arms to propel himself across the sea 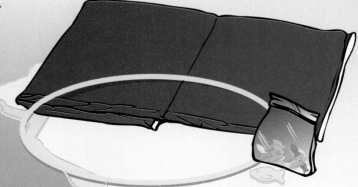 as if he were swimming—just as a polar bear does. Invite the swimming polar bear to swim into the sea to capture a bag of fish—his dinner. After he obtains his food, have him swim to another iceberg and give the rest mat to the child waiting there. Then have a child from the class replace the one who just completed his turn. Continue in this manner until every child has had the opportunity to swim the arctic sea in search of food. Throughout the activity, replenish the supply of polar bear food in the sea as necessary. When all your little swimmers have captured their food, invite them to enjoy the tasty treats they worked so hard to catch.

Polar Bear Parade

Invite your little ones to make polar bear masks to wear for a parade and during their arctic dramatic play. To make a mask, give each child a cutaway cup section of a cardboard egg carton. Have him paint the section black. After the paint dries, help the child glue the section to the center of a white paper plate to represent a polar bear's nose. Encourage the child to create ears and a mouth for his bear mask, using a variety of materials such as yarn, pipe cleaners, felt, and construction paper. Then assist him as necessary in cutting eyeholes from the paper plate. Use a hole puncher to punch a hole on each side of the mask; then thread a length of yarn through each hole and tie the yarn securely to the mask. To use, have a child position the mask in front of his face so that he can see out of the eyeholes. Then tie the loose ends of yarn together so that the mask fits snugly around his head. Have students line up; then turn on some marching music and invite youngsters to participate in a polar bear parade. Afterward encourage them to wear their masks as they pretend to be giant white bears that live and play around an imaginary North Pole.

I'm An Ice Bear!

Spark the imaginations of youngsters with a reading of *White Bear, Ice Bear* by Joanne Ryder (Mulberry Books). Then invite each child to pretend he has become a large ice bear just as the child did in the story. If desired, invite the students to put on their polar bear masks created in "Polar Bear Parade." Then have them perform the polar bear movements mentioned as the lines of this poem are recited.

Polar bear, polar bear, walk on the slippery snow.
Polar bear, polar bear, run around to and fro!

Polar bear, polar bear, take a dive deep down.
Polar bear, polar bear, swim and splash around.

Polar bear, polar bear, stand up, oh so tall!
Polar bear, polar bear, curl into a sleepy ball.

Hannah

Snowy Arctic Scenes

When youngsters create these snowy scenes, they will be able to demonstrate how they visualize the arctic landscape. Give each child a sheet of white paper on which to draw a small polar bear. Then have him cut out the bear and place it aside for later use. On a large sheet of light blue construction paper, have each student paint a wintry, arctic scene using white tempera paint and his choice of an applicator—a wide paintbrush, an old toothbrush, cotton swabs, or sponges. Encourage him to embellish his scene with painted icebergs, snowdrifts, snow caves, or even falling snow. After the paint dries, invite him to texturize his scene by gluing on materials such as small pieces of white, wrinkled tissue paper or packing foam. If desired, encourage the student to use dabs of iridescent paint to give his landscape a sun-sparkling, snowy appearance. When his scene is complete, have each child glue his polar bear onto it. Then frame each picture with black construction-paper strips. Display the snowy arctic scenes on a bulletin board titled "Polar Bears At Home."

A Polar Bear Booklet

These individual booklets will remind students of the neat characteristics of polar bears and provide them with information to share with their families. On white construction paper, reproduce the booklet backing on page 42 and the booklet pages on pages 44 and 45 for each child. Cut apart the booklet pages; then have youngsters complete each page and the backing as described. Sequence the completed pages on top of the booklet backing and staple them together.

- Page One: Draw snowflakes around the polar bear.
- Page Two: Draw black facial features on the polar bear.
- Page Three: Glue short, narrow strips of white tissue paper to the bottoms of the polar bear's feet.
- Page Four: Use blue tempera paint to sponge-paint water around the polar bear.
- Booklet Backing: Dictate three words to describe a polar bear.

My Polar Bear Book

Name: Carly

A polar bear's feet are big and nice. His furry feet grip the ice. 3

A polar bear swims in the sea. He's a much better swimmer than you or me! 4

Booklet Backing
Use with "A Polar Bear Booklet" on page 41.

My
Polar Bear
Book

Name: _____

©1996 The Education Center, Inc. • JANUARY • TEC211

A polar bear is

and

Staple book pages here.

Polar Bear Flannelboard Figures
Use with "A Giant White Bear" on page 36, "Where Is That Bear?" on page 37,
and "A Day In The Life Of A Polar Bear" on page 39.

swimming

walking

sleeping

smelling

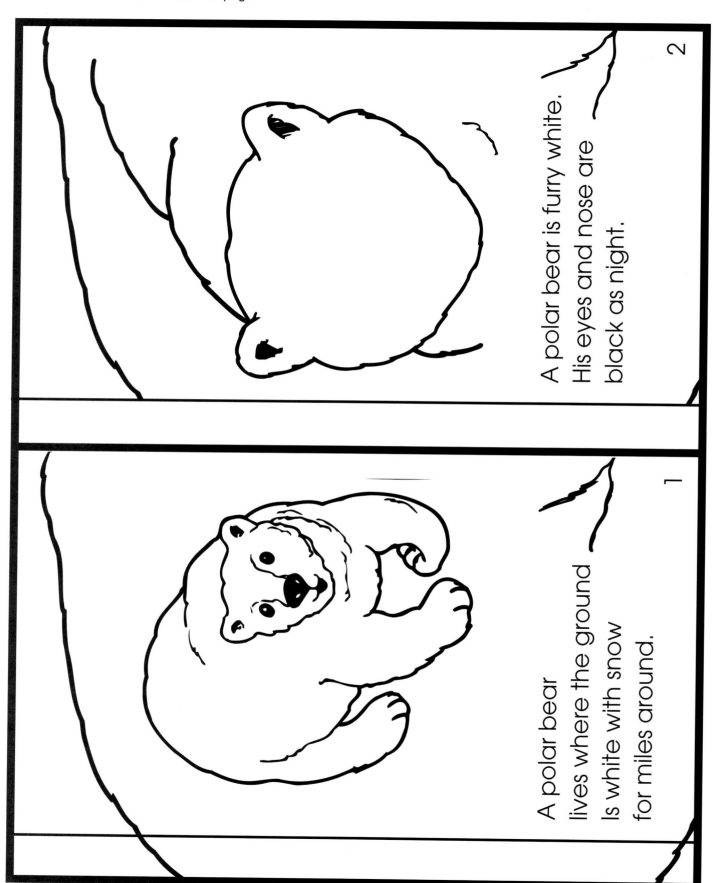

A polar bear is furry white.
His eyes and nose are black as night.

2

A polar bear
lives where the ground
Is white with snow
for miles around.

1

4

A polar bear
swims in the sea.
He's a much better swimmer
than you or me!

3

A polar bear's feet
are big and nice.
His furry feet grip the ice.

Eggs, Oatmeal, Cinnamon Bun— Breakfast Is A Lot Of Fun!

Wake up! It's time to learn about breakfast—that all-important, energizing meal that starts your day! Whether your little ones go for bacon or bagels, they're bound to eat up these breakfast ideas! *ideas contributed by Ada Hanley Goren and Pamela Priest*

A Breakfast Brainstorm

"What did you have for breakfast this morning?" Begin your breakfast unit by posing this simple-to-answer question to your little ones during circle time. Record the students' answers on the chalkboard or a sheet of chart paper. Draw a simple illustration of each food named to help nonreaders review the list. After everyone has had a turn to reply, ask youngsters to think of as many other breakfast foods as possible. Add these to your list. Then teach youngsters this fun song and the accompanying activity.

Good Morning, Let's Eat!
(sung to the tune of "Happy Birthday To You")

Good morning, let's eat!
Good morning, let's eat!
Let's have [cereal] for breakfast.
Good morning, let's eat!

Once students are familiar with the tune, encourage them to repeat the song, substituting other breakfast foods from the brainstormed list for the underlined word. Then add some action! Pass a plastic dish around the circle as you sing the song together. Each time you sing the third line of the song, the child holding the dish may name a breakfast food. When the group has finished singing that verse, lead the children in pretending to prepare and eat that breakfast food. For example, if a child names cereal, model the pouring of the imaginary cereal and milk and pretend to spoon the cereal into your mouth. Then continue passing the dish as you repeat the song for another imaginary meal.

46

Breakfast Buddies

Some things just go together—like eggs and bacon in a traditional American breakfast. Use the egg and bacon patterns on page 53 to help little ones find some more things that go together. Duplicate multiple copies of the egg patterns on yellow construction paper and the same number of bacon patterns on light brown construction paper. Cut out all the patterns; then program them to provide matching practice. For example, label each of 26 eggs with an uppercase letter and each of 26 bacon slices with a lowercase letter. Or label the cutouts to provide corresponding pairs for matching shapes, numerals and number words, or rhyming words. If desired, laminate all the pieces; then store them in a real frying pan. You've got a skills center that really sizzles!

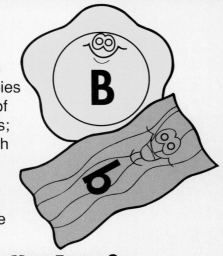

Which Flavor Do You Favor?

Present a nutritious breakfast food when you bring in some yogurt for your youngsters to sample. (Be sure to check for food allergies before proceeding.) First duplicate the recording sheet on page 52 for each child. Purchase—or have a parent donate—some large containers of vanilla yogurt and one bag each of frozen strawberries, blueberries, and peaches. For each child in a small group, prepare three small cups of yogurt. Pour the thawed fruit into three separate bowls. Then get ready for some "berry" fine taste testing!

Give each child his three cups of yogurt, a plastic spoon, and a recording sheet. Into one of each child's cups, stir a small spoonful of strawberries. Have him taste the yogurt; then ask him to draw a simple happy or sad face in the space above the strawberry on his recording sheet to indicate whether or not he liked this flavor. Repeat this procedure with other fruits. Encourage youngsters to count and compare how many children in the group liked and disliked each flavor. Then repeat the taste test with the remaining groups.

Mmmmm...Milk!

Yogurt isn't the only dairy food that's good for breakfast. Milk is an important part of a healthy breakfast for most children. Invite little ones to help you create a display to remind them of the benefits of drinking milk for breakfast. Print the following verse in the center of a sheet of poster board:

Milk in the morning each and every day
Makes my teeth and bones grow in a healthy way!
So start the day at breakfast with a glass or two.
Milk in the morning is oh-so-good for you!

After reading the poem aloud, serve each child a clear plastic cup of milk. (Be sure to check for food allergies first). Encourage her to make a milk mustache; then capture her resulting grin with an instant photo. Glue all the photos around the poem on the poster to finish off this silly—but significant—display.

47

Cereal Sorting

Packaged cereals are a popular breakfast choice for many children. So use this familiar food to help your little ones practice sorting and patterning skills. To prepare, purchase—or ask parents to send in—small boxes of round CheeriOs®, square Chex®, and rectangular Frosted Mini-Wheats®. Mix all the cereal together in a large bowl. Then, for each child, place a handful of the mixed cereal into a zippered plastic bag. Then duplicate the sorting sheet on page 52 for each child.

Encourage each youngster to open her bag and pour the cereal onto a paper towel. Have her sort the cereal by shape onto her sorting sheet. Ask questions to help your students explore concepts of *more, fewer,* and *equal,* as they count and compare the quantities of each cereal shape. Challenge more advanced students to make patterns with their cereal pieces—such as *square, square, circle, square, square, circle.* When the math practice is over, invite the children to use their math manipulatives as a cereal snack!

Oh My...Oatmeal!

Packaged cereals are popular all year, but sometimes cold winter mornings call for hot cereal. Inform your youngsters that January is Oatmeal Month; then invite them to join you in a circle-time oatmeal celebration! Seat the children in a circle and have them pass around an oatmeal canister to the rhythm of this chant. Repeat the chant several times, each time inviting a volunteer to replace the underlined word with the topping of his choice.

Oatmeal, oatmeal, in a dish,
What kind of topping do you wish?

Oatmeal, oatmeal, in a dish,
With [brown sugar] is what you wish!

Follow up this activity by having students create a class book. For each child, duplicate the class-book page on page 54 on white construction paper. Have each child cover the circle on his page first with glue, then with dry oatmeal. Provide a variety of art materials to represent oatmeal toppings—such as yarn, sticky dots, and construction-paper scraps. Write each child's dictated choice of oatmeal topping(s) on the blank line. Place each page in a separate zippered plastic bag; then stack the bagged pages and bind them along the left edge. For fun, roll up the book and store it in an empty oatmeal canister.

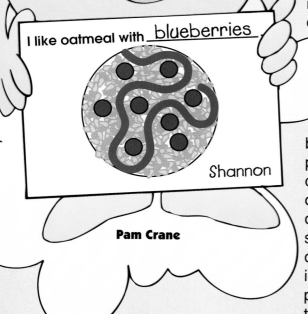

A **BIG** Bowl Of Oatmeal

Serve up a healthy portion of breakfast fun when you fill your sensory table with dry oatmeal. Place a variety of measuring cups, measuring spoons, and mixing bowls in the table as well. Encourage little ones to estimate how many cups or spoonfuls of oatmeal will fit into bowls of various sizes. Have them "write" their estimates and results in the oatmeal.

Toaster Tunes

Your little ones can start the day with a song when you teach them these lively tunes!

I'm A Little Toaster

(sung to the tune of "I'm A Little Teapot")

I'm a little toaster
With a slot.
Put in your bread
And I'll make it hot.
Push my little button;
Wait a while.
POP! Some toast
To make you smile!

Toast, Toast, Toast

(sung to the tune of "Row, Row, Row Your Boat")

Toast, toast, toast some bread
Golden brown and hot.
With butter and jam, bacon, or ham,
We like toast a lot!

Whip Up Some Waffles

Bring on the butter and syrup! It's time to do some breakfast cooking! Bring in all the ingredients to prepare your favorite waffle recipe, as well as a waffle iron. Let each youngster help in the preparation by mixing in an ingredient or stirring the waffle batter. Cook waffles for everyone. (Remember to use extra caution when working with electrical appliances in the classroom.) Serve the waffles with butter, syrup, and—if desired—fruit toppings or a dusting of powdered sugar.

After youngsters have devoured this tasty treat, gather them in your circle area and get out your chart paper and markers. Have the children dictate an experience story about preparing and eating the waffles. Use a different color of marker to write each individual sentence, being sure to note each child's name or initials next to his statement. After the story is finished, work together to think of an appropriate title. For more advanced students, you may want to consider this copy a first draft. Guide the children to organize the sentences to follow the actual sequence of the waffle-making experience. Print the final version on a clean sheet of chart paper.

Invite volunteers to illustrate the story in the margins of the chart paper before displaying it on a classroom wall or bulletin board.

Making Waffles

We put flour in a bowl.
Jeri

We added eggs and milk.
Robert

We cooked the waffles in a special machine.
Li

We put a lot of syrup on them and they were drippy.
Angelique

Michael
Westbury School

Out And About For Breakfast

Arrange to take your youngsters on a field trip that's a "hole" lot of fun—visit a doughnut or bagel shop! Make the trip a special event with these unique nametags. Cut round centers from a class supply of four-inch, construction-paper circles. Label each cutout with a child's name and your school's name. Then it's off to the shop to observe the machinery and processes involved in creating large batches of doughnuts or bagels. Be sure to request some free samples after your tour!

The Big Squeeze

This juicy idea will give your youngsters firsthand experience in preparing a popular breakfast beverage *and* strengthen their hand and finger muscles. To prepare, have parent volunteers send in a few bags of oranges. Borrow a pitcher, a strainer, and several handheld juicers. Slice the oranges in half; then set everything out on tables covered with bulletin-board paper. Have some disposable wipes on hand for cleaning up sticky fingers.

When all is ready, invite your students to a Juicin' Jamboree! Have students wash their hands before beginning. Demonstrate how to remove any visible seeds from an orange half; then place it on the juicer and twist it to extract the juice. Then encourage your little ones to join in on the juicing! After all the children have had a turn to use a juicer, pour all the collected juice through the strainer and into the pitcher. Invite each student to sample the freshly squeezed orange juice or store it in the refrigerator to serve later with a "Breakfast Buffet."

Breakfast Buffet

Ask moms and dads to be a part of your breakfast bonanza! Duplicate the invitation/request form on page 55 and send a copy home with each student. On the appointed day, arrange all the donated dishes—along with a supply of paper plates, napkins, and utensils—on a buffet table. Invite everyone to partake of the breakfast-foods feast. Share the projects your youngsters have completed during your breakfast unit with their proud parents. For some morning entertainment, encourage your little ones to give a performance of the "Toaster Tunes" from page 49!

The Best Breakfast

After sampling a variety of breakfast foods, each of your students probably has her own opinion as to what foods make the best breakfast. Show off students' choices with a simple-to-make bulletin-board display. Provide each child with a paper plate, a supply of magazines, and crayons. Invite her to cut pictures of her favorite breakfast foods from the magazines. Have her glue the pictures to her plate. If there is a food she is unable to find in a magazine, encourage her to draw it on the plate. Mount each plate on a bulletin board, along with a sentence strip bearing the child's name. Add the title "The Best Breakfast" to complete the display.

Amelia

Breakfast Around The World

After focusing your youngsters' attention on breakfast favorites in the United States, broaden their horizons with some information about breakfast in other parts of the world.

A Book About Breakfast

Locate the informative book, *Good Morning, Let's Eat!* by Karin Luisa Badt (Childrens Press®). As you show your youngsters the many photographs of people eating breakfast in other countries, paraphrase the text of the book or share these interesting breakfast facts with your young learners:

- In the United States, we consider certain foods breakfast foods and they are eaten primarily at breakfast time. In many cultures, people eat the same kinds of foods at any meal.
- The climate of a country may influence how much people eat for breakfast. People who live in warm-weather countries like to eat a light meal in the morning. People in countries with cold weather like a hearty meal to give them energy to stay warm.
- In some countries, sweet foods are favored for breakfast. In others, salty or tangy foods make up the morning meal.
- Breakfast foods vary widely. People eat pastries, cheese, salad, fish, beans, soup, and even hot dogs for breakfast!

Rice Vs. Rice Krispies®

Inform your students that in many cultures rice is a common dish on the breakfast table. (If you shared the book *Good Morning, Let's Eat!* in the activity "A Book About Breakfast," point out the pictures of people eating rice.) Tell youngsters that many packaged cereals that are popular in the United States are made from rice. Then invite students to taste and compare rice and rice-based cereal. Before your taste test, prepare two cutouts from bulletin-board paper—a bowl of rice and a cereal box. Label the bowl cutout "Rice" and the box cutout "Rice Krispies®." Prepare a title strip that reads "Which Tastes Better For Breakfast?" Mount the cutouts and title on a classroom wall.

Prepare a pot of warm white rice. Give each child a small serving of rice in a paper cup and a small serving of Rice Krispies® cereal and milk in a paper bowl. Provide each child with a spoon and invite her to taste the rice and the cereal. Then have her write her name or place a name card on either the bowl or the box cutout to indicate her preference. Together count the names on each cutout to determine how many children preferred each type of rice. Which taste does your class prefer?

Tanner Keesha
Curtis
Rice

Jason
Caroline
Kim
Tyler
Rice Krispies®

Record Sheet
Use with "Which Flavor Do You Favor?" on page 47.

Name _____

strawberry   blueberry   peach

Sorting Sheet
Use with "Cereal Sorting" on page 48.

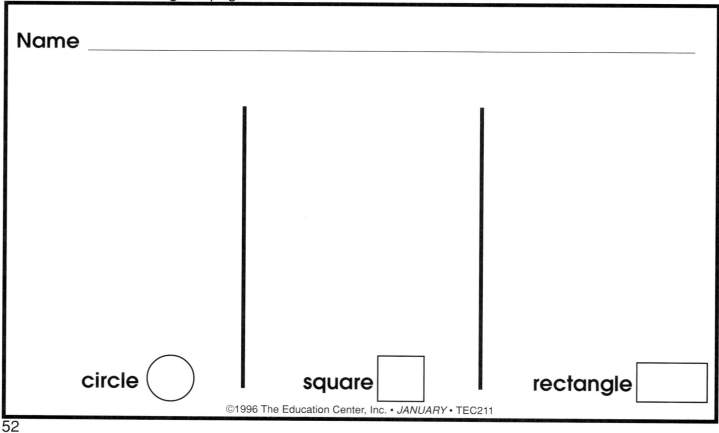

Name _____

circle   square   rectangle

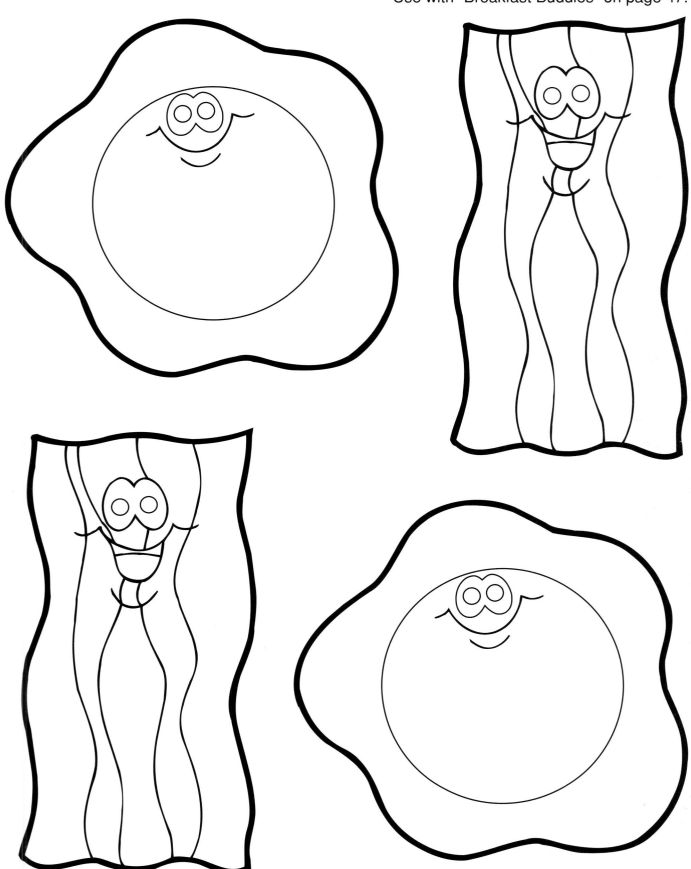

I like oatmeal with _____ .

54

©1996 The Education Center, Inc. • JANUARY • TEC211

Note To The Teacher: Use with "Oh My....Oatmeal!" on page 48.

Please Join Us For A Breakfast Buffet!

We've been learning about breakfast at school, and we'd love for you to come and eat breakfast with us!

Date: _____

Time: _____

Can you supply any of the breakfast foods or paper goods listed below?
Please let me know by _____.
(date)

scrambled eggs
bacon
yogurt
milk
cereal
oatmeal
toast
waffles
doughnuts or bagels
juice
paper plates
plastic spoons
plastic forks
paper cups

We hope to see you at our Breakfast Buffet!

Hand In Hand:
A Celebration Of Martin Luther King's Birthday

Dr. Martin Luther King, Jr., was a famous Black American who had a dream that someday all people would learn to love each other and live in harmony. His birthday is celebrated as a national holiday on the third Monday of January so that Americans will remember how his life touched the lives of millions. Place Dr. King's important message in the hands and hearts of your little ones with these ideas emphasizing love and friendship.

ideas contributed by Dayle Timmons

Dr. King's Dream

Give youngsters some basic information about who Dr. Martin Luther King, Jr., was and why we celebrate his birthday (see "Reading About Martin Luther King, Jr." on page 59 for some sources). Then read them this excerpt from his famous "I Have A Dream" speech:

"I have a dream that one day...little black boys and black girls will be able to join hands with little white boys and girls and walk together as sisters and brothers."

Explain to the children that Dr. King didn't mean a dream such as the ones we have when we are sleeping—but that the word *dream* can also mean a hope or a wish. Dr. King's hope was that all people would someday live together in harmony and friendship. Ask your students to stand in a circle; then teach them the first verse of this song.

He Had A Dream
(sung to the tune of "He's Got The Whole World In His Hands")

Verse 1

Martin Luther King, Jr., had a dream.
Martin Luther King, Jr., had a dream.
Martin Luther King, Jr., had a dream.
He had the whole world in his dream.
(Make a big circle with both hands.)

Verse 2

He had [Courtney] and [Wesley] in his dream.
He had [Kelly] and [Amanda] in his dream.
He had [Jimmie] and [Therese] in his dream.
He had the whole world in his dream.

After children have learned the first verse, sing the second verse, substituting two children's names in each line. Sing the children's names in the same order as they are standing in the circle, and explain that as each child hears her name, she should join hands with the children next to her. Continue in this manner until you have named everyone in the circle. Then sing the original verse again while everyone is holding hands.

Rainbow Of Dreams

Tell youngsters that Martin Luther King, Jr., gave a famous speech about his hope—or dream—for the future. Millions of people heard or have read his words about what the world might be like if people lived together in harmony. Invite youngsters to share their own dreams with all who visit your classroom when they help create this beautiful display. Duplicate page 60 for each child. Ask each student to draw a self-portrait in the open space at the bottom of his page. Then have him dictate his dream for the future for you to write in the dream cloud. Mount each child's paper on a sheet of construction paper.

To make a colorful centerpiece for the display, use a pencil to lightly outline the arc and stripes of a rainbow on a large sheet of white bulletin-board paper. Gather red, orange, yellow, green, blue, and purple tempera paints and a paintbrush for each color. Working with one child at a time, paint the child's hands; then direct him to press his hands onto the outlined rainbow. Have each child contribute a few handprints until the rainbow is complete with an arc in each color. Allow the paint to dry; then mount the rainbow on a bulletin board. Add the children's papers and a title strip that reads "Rainbow Of Dreams."

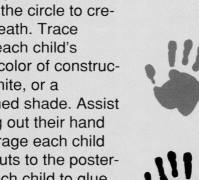

A "Hand-some" Wreath

In honor of Dr. King's birthday, decorate your classroom door with this lovely wreath. First cut a large circle from a sheet of poster board. Cut out the center of the circle to create a base for the wreath. Trace around each one of each child's hands on a different color of construction paper—black, white, or a multicultural, skin-toned shade. Assist the children in cutting out their hand shapes. Then encourage each child to glue his hand cutouts to the poster-board base. Invite each child to glue a red, construction-paper heart on the wreath. Finish the wreath by tying on a fluffy bow created with red, white, and black gift-wrapping ribbon.

RAINBOW OF DREAMS

I have a dream . . .

My Hand, Your Hand

In the spirit of Martin Luther King's beliefs, make a class book to show off the sameness that we all share, as well as the uniqueness of individuals. Take youngsters to your school's or center's copy machine. Ask each child to place one hand palm-down on the glass; then invite him to use his other hand to press the "copy" button to make a photocopy of his hand. Return to the classroom and assist each child in carefully cutting out his photocopied hand. Have each child glue his cutout to a sheet of white paper. On each child's paper, write "[Child's name]'s hand" below his cutout. Then give each child a small, red, construction-paper heart to glue on his hand picture. Stack all the pages and bind them between black construction-paper covers. On the front cover, use a white crayon to print the title "We'll Walk Hand In Hand." This book will become a hands-down favorite in your classroom reading center!

Joshua's hand

Heart Art

Reread Dr. King's words from his "I Have A Dream" speech (on page 56). Then invite each child to create this symbolic art project. Working with one small group at a time, give each child two sheets of construction paper— one light blue and one red. Use a paintbrush to paint a child's hands—one with black tempera paint and the other with white. Have the student make a paint handprint on each side of her sheet of light blue construction paper as shown. Then have her wash her hands. Provide her with a pair of scissors and demonstrate how to fold and cut her sheet of red construction paper to make a heart. Encourage her to glue the cut-out heart between her two handprints. Talk with the group about what the finished pictures symbolize—Dr. King's vision of love and friendship between people of different races.

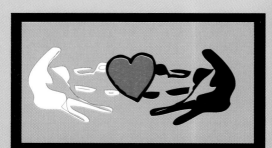

Birthday Bracelets

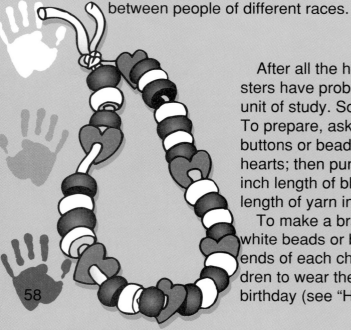

After all the holding, painting, tracing, and copying of hands, youngsters have probably surmised that their hands are a special part of this unit of study. So accentuate those hands with some special bracelets! To prepare, ask parents to donate a large supply of black and white buttons or beads. Cut a supply of small, red, construction-paper hearts; then punch a hole through the center of each heart. Cut a six-inch length of black or white yarn for each child. Dip one end of each length of yarn into glue and allow it to dry and harden overnight.

To make a bracelet, invite each child to string some black and some white beads or buttons and some paper hearts onto her yarn. Tie the ends of each child's length of yarn to fit her wrist. Encourage the children to wear their bracelets during a class celebration of Dr. King's birthday (see "Happy Birthday, Dr. King!" on page 59).

Happy Birthday, Dr. King!

Honor Martin Luther King, Jr., on this special day with a classroom birthday celebration! Dr. King's favorite foods were old-fashioned Southern favorites—such as fried chicken, sweet potatoes, black-eyed peas, and cornbread—so ask a few parents to donate these dishes for the celebration. Prepare some white and some chocolate cupcakes for students to decorate, as well.

Have each child ice the cupcake of her choice with either chocolate or vanilla frosting. Then invite her to add a few heart-shaped candies to the top of her cupcake. Lead youngsters in singing "Happy Birthday" to Dr. King before enjoying this festive feast!

Reading About Martin Luther King, Jr.

Although there have been many, many books written about Dr. King's life, only a few are appropriate for very young children. You may need to paraphrase the text of these selections for younger children, but these books will provide illustrations that will help youngsters get a sense of who Martin Luther King was and what he believed.

Happy Birthday, Martin Luther King
Written by Jean Marzollo
Published by Scholastic Inc.

A Picture Book Of Martin Luther King, Jr.
Written by David A. Adler
Published by Scholastic Inc.

Let Freedom Ring: A Ballad Of Martin Luther King, Jr.
Written by Myra Cohn Livingston
Published by Holiday House, Inc.

Martin Luther King Day
Written by Linda Lowery
Published by Carolrhoda Books

I Have A Dream...

Note To The Teacher: Use with "Rainbow Of Dreams" on page 57.

CALENDAR EXPLORATIONS

Kick off the new year by exploring calendar concepts with your youngsters. The following activities that focus on the concepts of *days, weeks,* and *months* will make your little ones anxious to conquer the calendar!

ideas contributed by Lucia Kemp Henry and Angie Kutzer

What's In A Year?

To help children better understand what makes a year, draw a diagram similar to the one shown on chart paper. Cut out the inside circle of seasons to use with this activity and cut the outer ring of months from the chart paper to use later in "A Circle Of Months." Explain that long ago people used the sun, moon, and stars to tell them when to plant food and when to get ready for cold weather. They noticed that certain types of weather kept happening over and over. What they actually discovered was the cycle of the seasons! Display your circle of seasons and discuss this cyclic pattern. Because our calendar year starts with January, start with winter and point out that each complete pass around the circle equals one year. Ask children to draw pictures of activities they do during certain seasons. Then glue their work onto a round mural divided into fourths. Attach the circle of seasons to the center of your mural so that it can be removed easily for use with "A Circle Of Months."

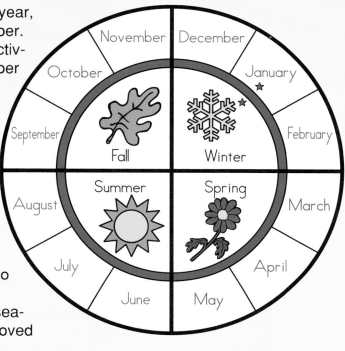

A Circle Of Months

Use the circle of seasons from "What's In A Year?" and attach the outer ring of months, lining up the two stars. Point to each month, say its name, and tell popular events and holidays that occur during that month. Then use this song and the accompanying motions with the month cards on page 65 (for picture cues) to have your youngsters going mad about months!

(sung to the tune of "Twinkle, Twinkle, Little Star")

Twelve months in a year, it's true.
Let me say them all for you.
January brings the snow. *(Shake and shiver.)*
February—hearts aglow. *(Point to heart.)*
March roars in and then it's spring. *(Jump and cheer.)*
April showers make us sing. *(Arms up and fingers wiggle down like rain.)*

Twelve months in a year, it's so.
We have eight more months to go.
May makes flowers bloom and sway. *(Wave arms.)*
June has Father's special day. *(Swing a bat and hug yourself.)*
July 4th the fireworks blast. *(Flash hands in the air.)*
August comes and summer's past. *(Sad face and thumbs-down.)*

Twelve months in a year, it's so.
We have four more months to go.
In September—friends to meet. *(Wave to others.)*
In October—"Trick or treat!" *(Hold bag open for candy.)*
In November—pumpkin pies. *(Rub tummy.)*
In December—Santa flies. *(Point, and look up and across sky.)*

Twelve months in a year, it's true.
We have named them all for you!

61

Month Memory

Promote spatial visualization and memory skills by playing Concentration with the months! Enlarge and make two copies of the reproducible on page 65 for a whole-group game, or duplicate two copies per child on construction paper for partner and take-home practice. Whether you decide to play Concentration as a group, in pairs, or individually, your children will love their little calendar squirrel...each and every month of the year!

Break It On Down

Begin this activity by showing your children a 12-month calendar. (Any hanging calendar will do as long as it has 12 pages.) Let the children count the months as you flip the pages. Ask them what 12 months equals. Then tear out a page. Ask what you are holding. Explain that a *month* is made up of *weeks.* Point out what a week is and count the weeks in that month. Cut a week out of the month. Hold it up and ask what it is. Count how many squares it takes to make a week. Explain that these squares are called *days* and point to each square while naming a day. The children should be able to say the days of the week with you and some may even want to say them solo! Afterward march around the room or playground, military-style, chanting this responsive rhyme to the rhythm of "Sound Off":

Sunday, Monday, and Tuesday; *(teacher)*
Sunday, Monday, and Tuesday; *(children)*
Wednesday, Thursday, and Friday; *(teacher)*
Wednesday, Thursday, and Friday; *(children)*
Saturday is the week's end. *(teacher)*
Saturday is the week's end. *(children)*
Then it's time to start again. *(teacher)*
Then it's time to start again. *(children)*
Sound off! *(teacher)*
1! 2! *(children)*
Sound off! *(teacher)*
3! 4! *(children)*
Break it on down: *(teacher)*
1, 2, 3, 4, 1, 2,...**3! 4!** *(children)*

Month Munchies

Take a bite out of the calendar! Prepare a 9" x 13" sheet cake and frost it with white icing. Use two small tubes of colored frosting gel to draw the month of January on the cake: one color for the grid and one for the writing. Show the cake to your children and review the calendar terms being studied—*month, week,* and *day.* To serve the cake, cut it along the grid lines. Before lifting out each child's square, discuss with him the day of the week it represents and its numeral. As students are enjoying their treat, share a good calendar story from the booklist on page 63.

Calendar Connections

Cookie's Week
Written by Cindy Ward
Published by Scholastic Inc.

Come Out And Play, Little Mouse
Written by Robert Kraus
Published by Greenwillow Books

Seven Blind Mice
Written by Ed Young
Published by Scholastic Inc.

A Busy Year
Written by Leo Lionni
Published by Scholastic Inc.

Line 'em Up!

Practice sequencing and matching skills by using the days of the week. To prepare, use 14 sentence-strip halves and label two for each day of the week. Read the book *All Year Long* by Nancy Tafuri (Greenwillow Books) to your children. This book combines days and months in sequence as it beautifully illustrates characteristics of the months and special events of the year. After reading the story, use the sentence strips to improve students' sequencing and matching abilities. Display one set of days in order for your students to use as a reference. Hand out the other set of days to seven children. Have this group come forward and attempt to put themselves in order, matching their cards to the ones on display. Read the resulting lineup with your remaining children and allow the sentence-strip holders to rearrange themselves if necessary. Once the order of the days is correct, ask the group of children up front to give the cards to other children for a try.

Weekly Happenings

Strengthen your children's concept of a week by relating it to their own experiences. If you already have a schedule posted, make it "kid-friendly" by attaching picture cues for weekly activities—a palette for art, a ball for recess, a book for library, etc. If you don't already have a display, make a classroom banner of the class's weekly routine. Accordion-fold a seven-foot length of bulletin-board paper into one-foot sections; then unfold it. Label each section with a day of the week and ask students to draw or find magazine pictures (supply catalogs are a good source) of activities held weekly. Glue these pictures on the correct days on the banner and label them to indicate the activities represented. Ask children questions about the week: "What day do we go to the library [art, computer lab, etc.]?" Be sure to throw in a few tricky ones for a little critical thinking: "What day do we go to lunch?" or "What do we do on Thursday?" Once your students get the hang of it, have them ask the questions. Post the banner and children can see at a glance their activities for the day and week.

Planning Ahead

Expose your youngsters to a very valuable habit—planning ahead. In preparation, duplicate class copies of January's calendar and make a transparency for your use. (Depending on your age group, have the calendar already numbered or let your students numerate their own.) Model on your transparency how to start at the beginning of the month and travel left-to-right and top-to-bottom through the month—highlighting birthdays, holidays, special events, and vacation days with simple drawings, stickers, or stamps. Have your students do the same to their calendars.

Take five minutes at the end of each day during the month to pull out the calendars and have children cross out the day just finished. Also have them add any special events that have come up unexpectedly and count the days until the next happening. This activity reinforces the directionality of reading while giving your students some things to look forward to.

Work-Of-Art Calendars

Create calendars that are showplaces for student artwork, and they'll definitely get a lot of attention. To make a calendar, begin by attaching a press-on pocket or a zippered plastic bag to the upper half of a 10" x 16" tagboard rectangle. To make this calendar especially appealing, program blank, numbered calendar grids (for the remainder of the school year) to indicate the birthdays of classmates, school holidays, and special events; then photocopy each calendar for each youngster. Sequence the photocopies, hole-punch them, and attach them to the lower half of the tagboard. Punch a hole near the top of the tagboard for hanging the calendar. When you have prepared a calendar for each student, have him select a piece of his recent artwork that he especially enjoys. Trim it to fit inside the pocket or bag attached to his calendar; then slip the artwork inside. Not only will these calendars be considered masterpieces, but they also can be displayed at home where parents and children can talk about upcoming events in the school year. Periodically trim students' artwork to fit their calendars; then send the artwork home, suggesting that students replace the original masterpiece.

JANUARY

FEBRUARY

MARCH

APRIL

MAY

JUNE

JULY

AUGUST

SEPTEMBER

OCTOBER

NOVEMBER

DECEMBER

Character Lessons

Enter the land of make-believe with your youngsters when you explore this treasure trove of time-honored traditional tales. On your journey, little ones will meet lots of interesting characters *and* learn some character-building lessons along the way.

ideas contributed by Lucia Kemp Henry and Mackie Rhodes

Tale-Telling Tips

The repetitive lines and actions found in some fairy tales lend themselves well to student participation in the story's telling and retelling. Use your preferred version of *The Three Little Pigs, The Three Billy Goats Gruff, Goldilocks And The Three Bears,* and *The Little Red Hen* to present each story to little ones. Then select some of the ideas listed to involve your students in retelling one or all four of these classic stories.

• Write some of the repetitive lines from a story on a sheet of chart paper. As you reach these lines in a retelling of the story, invite youngsters to chorally chant the lines with you. Or, if several characters have repetitive lines, assign a different character's part to a different group of children to say during the storytelling.

"Little pig, little pig, Let me come in!"

• Set up your dramatic-play area to entice youngsters to reenact each story. Provide props—such as character masks, furniture, and story items—for students to use as they assume the roles of story characters. Have small groups of children use the props to act out the story and add their own versions of events as they desire.

• Invite small groups of children to work together to create a simplified play version of each story. Encourage them to work out part assignments, staging, costumes, and props.

• Encourage students to create their own books to tell a fairy tale. Provide youngsters with a supply of paper and a variety of drawing utensils. Invite them to dictate and illustrate their own versions of one, or even all, of the stories. Then bind each book and place it in a reading center. Ask each student to share his story with at least one classmate.

• Have students prepare fairy-tale puppets, flannelboard figures, or stand-up figures (as described in "Fairy-Tale Fun" on page 67) for any or all of the stories; then invite them to use the figures to tell their versions of each story.

After-The-Facts Snacks

After sharing each of the fairy tales with youngsters, invite them to enjoy the snack listed to represent each story.

• *The Three Little Pigs:* Serve Chinese noodles, potato sticks, and crackers to represent straw, sticks, and bricks. If desired, also include marshmallow puffs.

• *The Three Billy Goats Gruff:* Serve seasoned oriental noodles tinted with green food coloring to represent grass.

• *Goldilocks And The Three Bears:* Serve cooled oatmeal, grits, or Cream Of Wheat®. If desired, provide honey or syrup for youngsters to put in their porridge.

• *The Little Red Hen:* Give each student a slice of bread. Invite him to spread butter and jelly on his bread with a plastic knife.

From Fairy-Tale Characters

Fairy-Tale Fun

Using fairy-tale figures can provide lots of learning and role-playing fun for little ones. Use the reproducible fairy-tale patterns on pages 72–75 to make some of the following; then encourage students to use the figures for any of the following activities.

- Color tagboard copies of the character patterns; then laminate them if desired. Tape each character to a craft stick to create a stick puppet. Invite youngsters to use the puppets to tell the tale.

- Glue the reproduced character patterns to separate pieces of foam-core boards. Create a stand for each figure from a piece of Styrofoam®. Invite youngsters to use the stand-up figures to tell the story.

- Reproduce several copies of the character figures on construction paper. Color and laminate the figures; then cut them out. Have a child use the figures for sorting, patterning, and counting activities.

- Enlarge the character figures; then invite youngsters to make simple, paper-bag puppets with the figures. Encourage the children to use their puppets to tell the story.

Take-Home Totes

Have youngsters make these special envelopes to hold their take-home fairy-tale materials. Provide each child with a large kraft envelope programmed across the top with "This Fairy-Tale Tote Belongs To: _____." Have each child write his name on the line; then invite him to decorate both sides of the envelope with illustrations representing any or all of the fairy tales in this unit. If desired, laminate the envelopes; then use a craft knife to slit the top opening of each envelope. Inside each envelope include a note suggesting ways in which the parent and child can use the enclosed fairy-tale items.

- Have youngsters color enlarged tagboard copies of the character figures. Laminate the figures; then encourage children to cut them apart to make puzzles. Have a student assemble a puzzle, then tell something about the character.

- Display the enlarged fairy-tale patterns on a bulletin board. Write the students' dictated version of each story on a separate sheet of chart paper and display each with the corresponding patterns.

- Encourage little ones to take home a reproduced page of fairy-tale figures to share with their families. Ask them to include another family member in coloring, cutting out, and using the figures to retell the story.

- Enlarge the fairy-tale patterns to a desired size; then make tagboard flannelboard figures for each story. Back each figure with the hook side of a piece of Velcro®. Use the figures as you tell the story. Or invite youngsters to manipulate the figures while they tell their own story versions.

This Fairy Tale Tote Belongs To ___Jay___ .

The Three Little Pigs

This porcine tale that teaches how planning and hard work pay off is a perennial favorite of many little ones. Even the wolf, with his persistent puffing, has a valuable lesson to teach youngsters! Supplement your storytelling and student renditions of this popular tale with some character-building activities that are sure to make a lasting impression on youngsters!

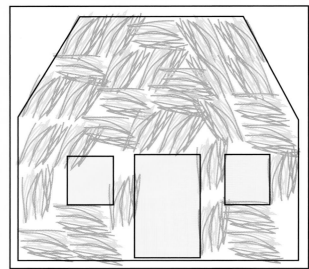

Building Cooperation

As youngsters plan and work together to build these examples of the pigs' houses, they will also be building important skills in relating to others. Draw a large, simple house on each of three lengths of white bulletin-board paper. Divide your students into three groups; then provide each group with a house drawing and a different type of material with which to decorate the house. For instance, have one group create a straw house by gluing real straw or raffia to their house. Have another group glue brown construction-paper strips or real twigs to their drawing. For the brick house, encourage students to sponge-paint bricks or glue corrugated-paper bricks onto their drawing. Before beginning, encourage each group of students to devise a plan to divide the task of "building" its house. For example, some students might work on the door while others work on the roof or walls. After the houses have been completed, ask each group to share their building plan and to comment on its efficiency. Which child "built" which part of the house? Did the plan work well? Then display the completed houses in the dramatic-play area as scenery for role-playing the story.

Huffing And Puffing

Little ones will be intrigued to learn that even the big, bad wolf has some good character traits! Explain to youngsters that the wolf is a persistent, clever fellow—he doesn't give up easily when he sets his mind on a goal. In many versions of this story, it was only when the wolf was certain that he could *not* achieve his goal (capturing a pig for his supper) that he stopped trying—but not before making several resourceful attempts! Invite students to do some persistent puffing with this activity that challenges them to continue striving for a goal. To prepare, place a few lightweight items on

the floor—such as a cotton ball, a wrinkled piece of tissue paper, and a foam ball. Then turn a box on its side and place it a distance from the items. Ask each child in turn to lie on the floor and blow one of the items across the room toward the box. Encourage him to continue blowing the item, staying close to it by moving forward, until he accomplishes his goal—blowing the item into the box. Then ask each child to find another way to get the item into the box without the use of his hands. How many different ways can the students think of? Youngsters will amaze themselves with their own persistence and resourcefulness—and they may even find they have some respect for that big, bad wolf!

The Three Billy Goats Gruff

Use the character examples in this classic tale to bridge some lasting lessons about courage, patience, responsibility, problem solving, and self-discipline for youngsters.

I am brave when I ride the schoolbus.

We Call On Our Courage

We Call On Our Courage

Each of the Billy Goats Gruff demonstrated courage and resourcefulness as he stepped foot onto the bridge to face the mean troll. But, as the largest goat waited patiently for his turn to cross, he knew that the safety and well-being of his younger brothers was his responsibility—he must have had brave determination to prevent the troll from harming any of them! After telling this tale and sharing the positive character traits of the goats, ask each student to think of a circumstance in which he needed to demonstrate courage—such as riding the bus on the first day of school, going to the dentist, or eating a new food. Give each child the opportunity to tell about his courageous moment. Then provide each child with a large sheet of white construction paper to illustrate a situation in which he showed bravery. Write his dictated statement about his picture on the page. Then bind the stacked pages together between two construction-paper covers. Title the book "We Call On Our Courage" and place it in the reading center to provide some inspirational reading for students.

The Troll's Good Traits

Although the troll under the bridge may seem mean and uncaring, he does have a few things to teach us all—problem solving and self-discipline are his strong suits! Explain to youngsters that the troll was able to tell by sound which goat crossed his bridge—the small, medium, or large goat. Since each of the first two goats made the promise of a larger goat following soon after, the troll delayed satisfying his cravings by waiting for a bigger, meatier goat to capture for his meal—a prime example of self-discipline! After discussing some of the troll's finer points, invite youngsters to role-play his character and problem-solving abilities. Ask a volunteer to be the troll. Have her turn her back to the other students. Then place several instruments behind the troll. Have another child select one of the instruments. Have that child walk back and forth behind the troll, striking the instrument to represent the sound of trip-trapping goat hooves. (Encourage the troll to practice some self-discipline by resisting the temptation to turn around and look for the noisemaker!) Have the child replace the instrument; then ask the troll to turn around and determine which instrument was used to make the sound effects. During the activity, remind the other students to follow the troll's example of self-discipline by waiting patiently for their turns. Exchange instruments in and out of the lineup as different children have the opportunity to role-play the troll and goat.

Goldilocks And The Three Bears

Compassion and respect—these are just two of the many character lessons that youngsters can learn from these activities centered around this furry trio of bears and their golden-haired visitor.

The Caring Bears

Have you ever wondered what the outcome of this story would be had the three bears shown some concern and compassion for Goldilocks rather than frightening her away? Ask youngsters to contemplate this question; then invite them to role-play the story in reverse sequence, giving it a compassionate twist. Have four students each assume a role for a different character in the story. Begin the role-playing with the three bears discovering Goldilocks asleep in Baby Bear's bed. Prompt the bears to awaken the girl and ask her questions about her well-being—such as "Are you sick?" and "Are you comfortable?" Then have the bears and Goldilocks move to the scene of the broken chair. Encourage the bears to show concern for the girl by making statements such as "I hope you didn't get hurt" and "You must have felt bad when the chair broke." While at the kitchen scene, the bears might make compassionate remarks such as "You must have been very hungry" and "I hope you had enough to eat." Finally ask the bears to demonstrate their concern for Goldilocks' being alone in the woods with comments such as "You must have been afraid" and "I'm glad you felt safe in our house." After all the students have taken part in the role-playing, encourage them to practice compassion in their play and daily activities.

Puzzled Apologies

Now that the three bears have demonstrated so much care and concern for her, Goldilocks has only one course of action to take—to apologize! After all, she did enter the bears' home and use their personal items without permission. As students role-play the story, encourage Goldilocks to express her apologies for her wrongdoings and perhaps even state a more acceptable substitute for her behaviors—such as not entering the house when not invited, or asking for permission to use personal items. Then invite youngsters to make these apology puzzles. For each child, duplicate an enlarged copy of the small chair figure on page 74 on tagboard. Have each child color and cut out the chair; then ask him to draw a picture of Goldilocks on the back of the cutout. Help the student write "I'm sorry" near his illustration and enclose the words with a speech bubble. Laminate each cutout; then have each child cut his chair picture into a three- to five-piece puzzle. Invite student partners to assemble each other's puzzles. Then place each puzzle in a zippered storage bag to send home. Encourage students to challenge their family members to assemble their puzzles and to share their own versions of this fairy tale.

The Little Red Hen

From the classic example of this story's main character, youngsters will learn that industriousness and self-reliance reap a heap of satisfaction! And, although the hen worked alone, little ones can still learn a lesson about the rewards of being helpful.

All By Myself

The self-reliant hen demonstrates perfectly how internal motivation and direction lead to positive and rewarding results. Explain to youngsters that the hen could have chosen to do nothing with the seeds that she found. Instead she decided to plant them. This, in turn, led to a chain of events that required the hen to choose either to continue working diligently toward a goal or to quit. In each situation, the hen relied on her work ethic and determination to see the task through. Then she enjoyed the fruits of her labor—a delicious loaf of bread! Invite students to demonstrate some self-reliance and self-direction with this activity. Gather a large variety of materials—blocks, puzzles, interactive books, and any other items that can be used independently by a child. From this assortment, have each child choose one activity. Then set a kitchen timer for up to ten minutes. Encourage each child to quietly use the materials of his choice for that period of time. After the timer rings, praise youngsters for keeping themselves interested and busy with their activities. Your little ones may amaze you with their internal drive and independence!

Help! I Need Somebody!

The little red hen was a hard worker, no doubt. However, her tasks would certainly have been made easier if only her friends had been willing to pitch in and help. Use this activity to provide students with a lesson on being helpful—and on appreciating the help they receive. In baseball-diamond fashion, arrange a cup, a bowl, a large, plastic margarine container, and a shoebox on the floor. Nearly fill each of the first three containers with packing peanuts or cotton balls to represent wheat. Then divide your class into groups of four students. Have each student in a group assume one of the character roles from the story. Explain that one child will use her hands to scoop out all the wheat from the cup and transfer it to the bowl. If she needs help to make the transfer, one other child—a friend—from her group may help. Then those two friends will transfer the wheat from the bowl to the margarine container. Again, if help is needed, one additional friend from the group may help. Finally the children will transfer all the wheat to the shoebox—employing the assistance of all their group's friends. After the job is completed, encourage group members to share their appreciation and congratulations with one another for a job well done. Taking part in this exercise will surely help youngsters understand the value of giving and receiving help.

Story Patterns: *The Three Little Pigs*

Use with "Fairy-Tale Fun" on page 67.

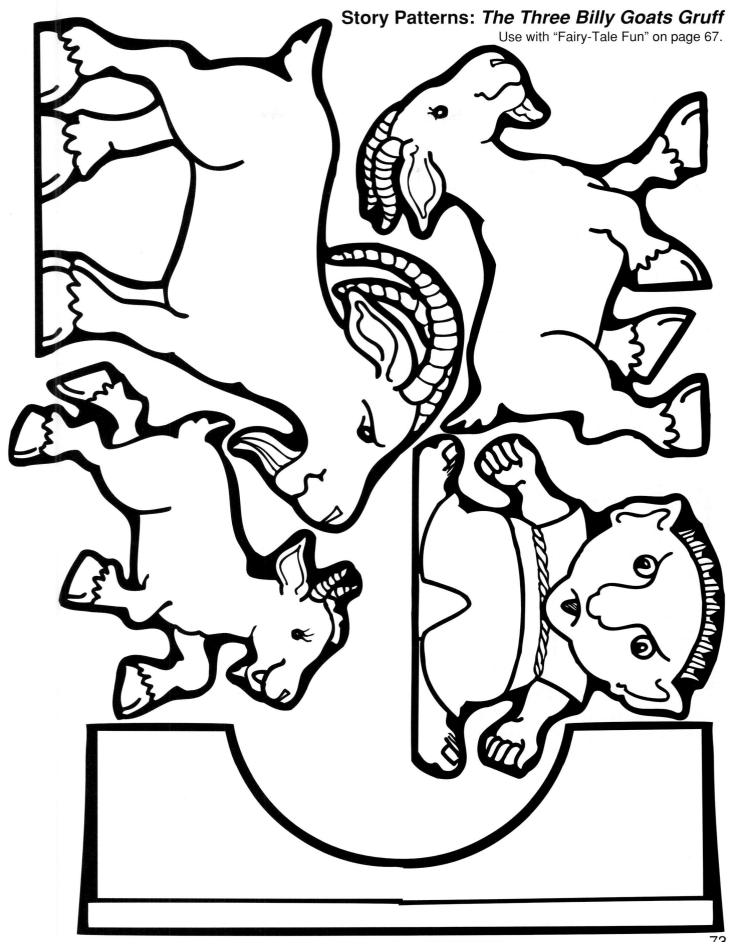

Our Phenomenal Prehistoric Pals

Ever since the first dinosaur fossil was identified in 1822, people of all ages have been fascinated by the wonder, mystery, and curiosity surrounding these phenomenal creatures. Invite youngsters to make their own discoveries about these prehistoric animals while having some roaring good fun learning "dino-mite" facts!

ideas contributed by Suzanne Moore and Mackie Rhodes

The Experts

Most likely, your youngsters will know bits and pieces of information about dinosaurs—but do they know how this information was gathered? Explain to students that most of our knowledge of dinosaurs is a result of the work of *paleontologists*. These scientists learn about prehistoric life by studying fossils that have been buried in layers of rock. Dinosaur experts can estimate the sizes of dinosaurs and determine their eating habits by measuring the sizes of fossilized bones, footprints, and teeth. They can also put together a dinosaur skeleton on a metal frame to resemble what they think the real animal looked like.

Ask your little ones to imagine that they are paleontologists. Have them share what they know about dinosaurs with the class. Record their comments and statements on a large dinosaur cutout. Then display this cutout with the title "What We Know About Dinosaurs."

Dinosaurs are big.
Dinosaurs have sharp teeth.
They lived a long time ago.

Colossal Fossils

Paleontologists know that a fossil forms from an impression left by a part of a plant or an animal that lived millions of years ago. Over time, the impression hardens into rock, and a permanent imprint is left behind. To help youngsters understand how a fossil forms, invite them to make their own fossils. Then use these student-made fossils to challenge youngsters' reasoning and matching skills.

To make mud for 6–8 fossils, thoroughly mix together 2 cups of flour, 1 cup each of water and salt, and 6 tablespoons of dry brown tempera paint. For each child, place a shallow layer of the fossil mud into a container, such as a small, foil pie pan or Styrofoam® meat tray. Have each child smooth the surface of his mud, then firmly press an object—a shell, stick, plastic dinosaur model, or plastic leaf, or any other object that will leave an impression—into the mud to create a fossil imprint. Set the imprinted mud aside to dry for several days. Collect, clean, and dry all the objects used to make the imprints; then place them in a container and set it aside for later use in this activity.

After the mud fossils dry, remove them from their containers. Spread the fossils out on a table; then place the container of objects used for the fossil imprints nearby. Invite children to take turns matching each object to its fossil imprint. Your young paleontologists may really make an impression on you with their colossal fossil-matching skills!

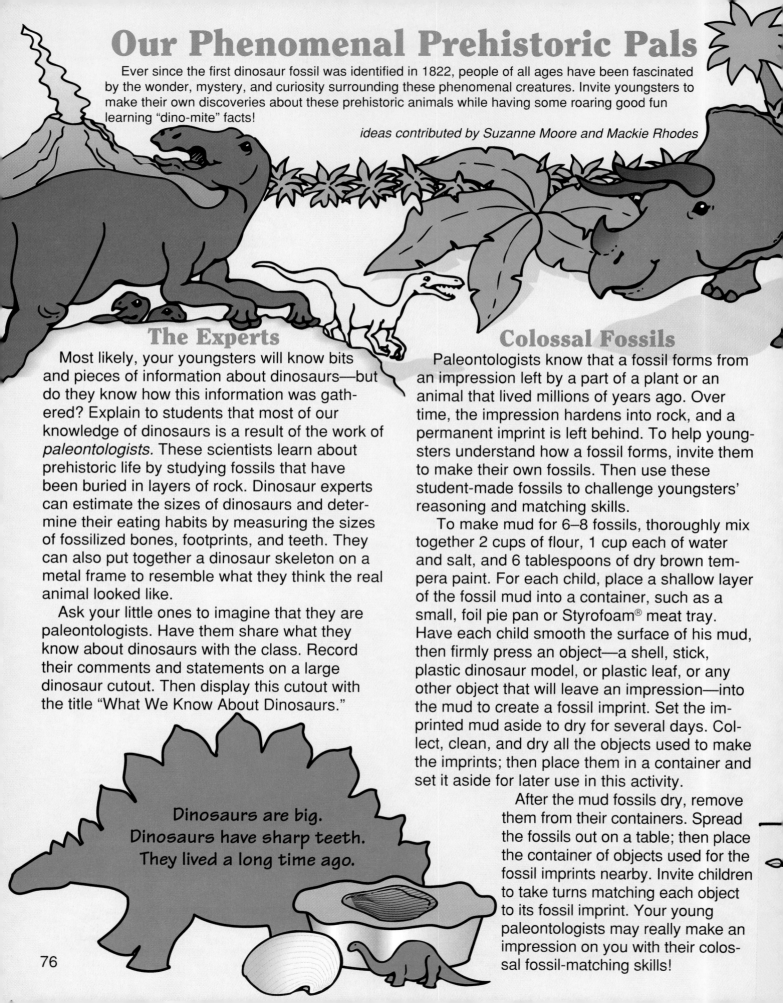

The Search Is On

Now that your little ones have some understanding of how fossils are formed (see "Colossal Fossils" on page 76), invite them to role-play paleontologists in search of fossils. Prepare a dig site for students using your class sand table. To do this, partially fill the table with wet sand; then bury in the sand some of the fossils created in "Colossal Fossils" on page 76. Provide a small group of youngsters with tools—such as plastic hand shovels, craft sticks, toothpicks, six-inch rulers, and small brushes. Encourage youngsters to use the tools to find and remove the fossils from the dig site. Caution students to handle each fossil with care—it is a rare and precious find! After each student has dug up a fossil, invite him to clean it using the available tools; then have him sketch a picture of his find on a sheet of paper. Label each child's illustration with the name of the fossil. If desired, stack the pages between two construction-paper covers and bind them along the left edge to make a class book. Title the book "Our Fossil Finds." Place the class book in the reading center for student partners to enjoy reading.

Bony Connections

Them bones, them bones, them dinosaur bones! So what does a paleontologist do with all those dinosaur bones that he finds? He sets to work assembling them into a dinosaur skeleton. He then uses his knowledge about dinosaurs to determine what kind of skeleton has been discovered. Invite your youngsters to do some paleontological problem solving with this bare-bones activity. In advance, duplicate the dinosaur skeletons flannelboard figures on page 82 on white construction paper. Mount the skeletons on a sheet of tagboard. Cut out each skeleton; then laminate the cutouts. Attach the hook side of a piece of self-adhesive Velcro® to the back of each cutout. Then read aloud *Digging Up Dinosaurs* by Aliki (Harper & Row, Publishers). Afterward invite youngsters to imagine that they are paleontologists. Ask them to decide which dinosaur fits each of these descriptions as the skeleton of that dinosaur is displayed on the flannelboard. If desired, send a copy of the dinosaur skeletons home with each child to share with his family.

- Bony plates extend from the back and tail of this dinosaur's skeleton. It has a big, heavy body. A beak is at the front of its small, narrow head. Its front legs are shorter than its back legs. Two pairs of bony spikes are at the end of its tail. *(Stegosaurus)*

- This 70-foot-long, plant-eating dinosaur has long, thin teeth and a small, slender head. Its straight, thick, front legs are shorter than its hind legs. Its long tail ends in a slender point. *(Apatosaurus)*

- One short, thick horn on its nose and two sharp horns over its eyes are found on the enormous head of this dinosaur. It has a turtle-like beak. A bony shield, called a *frill,* extends from the back of its skull. Thick, strong legs support its heavy, 25-foot-long body. *(Triceratops)*

- The teeth of this strong, meat-eating dinosaur measure about six inches long. It has very short forelimbs and long hind legs. It is about 40 feet in length. *(Tyrannosaurus)*

- This small meat-eater has a narrow, birdlike head and long legs and feet. It is about the size of a chicken. *(Compsognathus)*

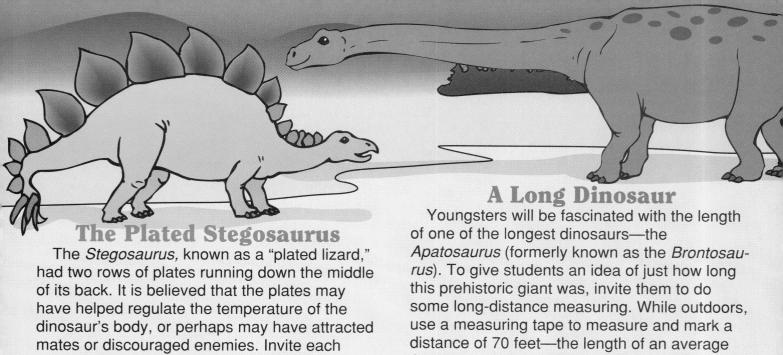

The Plated Stegosaurus

The *Stegosaurus,* known as a "plated lizard," had two rows of plates running down the middle of its back. It is believed that the plates may have helped regulate the temperature of the dinosaur's body, or perhaps may have attracted mates or discouraged enemies. Invite each youngster to create a model of a Stegosaurus using a plate familiar to him—a paper plate! To make a Stegosaurus, have each child choose a color to sponge-paint a paper plate and a cut-away row of cardboard egg-carton cups. After the paint dries, have him cut his paper plate in half. Along the curved edge of one of the paper-plate halves, help the child staple the egg-cup strip (a strip of egg-crate foam—available at some fabric stores—may be substituted) so that it resembles the body of a Stegosaurus. Then have the student cut away the fluted edge of the other paper-plate half and attach it to one end of the body to represent its tail. Help the child as needed to cut out a Stegosaurus head and four legs from the remaining piece of paper plate. Have the child glue the head and legs to his Stegosaurus's body; then invite him to draw in facial features and to cut slits at the end of the tail to create spikes. Display the completed dinosaurs with the title "Look What's On Our Plates!"

A Long Dinosaur

Youngsters will be fascinated with the length of one of the longest dinosaurs—the *Apatosaurus* (formerly known as the *Brontosaurus*). To give students an idea of just how long this prehistoric giant was, invite them to do some long-distance measuring. While outdoors, use a measuring tape to measure and mark a distance of 70 feet—the length of an average Apatosaurus. Divide your class into small groups of students; then have each group measure and cut a piece of yarn the same length as the marked distance. (If you prefer to use shorter lengths, have students measure yarn to equal the length of the dinosaur's 30-foot tail or 20-foot neck.) Then encourage each group to use its yarn-length to measure some outdoor distances—such as the distance from the door to the playground equipment, or the length of the sidewalk along one side of your school. Record the number of yarn-lengths needed for each distance as a child from each group reports this information. Afterward share with the class the number of Apatosauruses that could stand head-to-tail for each measured distance. Invite the students to pace out each of these distances. To further emphasize the length of these dinosaurs, and for additional practice in measurement, have students use their yarn-lengths to measure indoor distances. Ask them to determine whether an Apatosaurus would be shorter or longer than a specified distance. This simple measurement activity sure goes a long way!

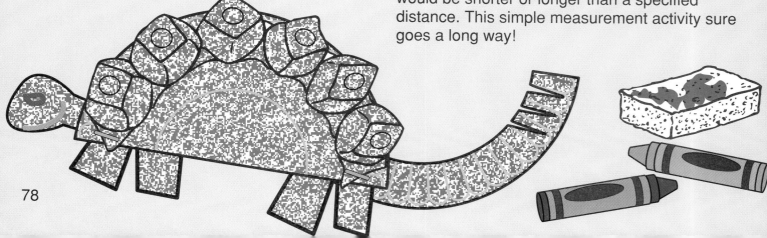

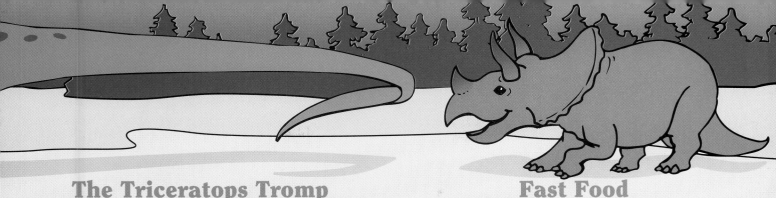

The Triceratops Tromp

The three horns that extended from its head were the most prominent feature of a *Triceratops*. Even the dinosaur's name means "three-horned face." Use this fast-action sorting activity to help youngsters remember the number three in association with the Triceratops's three horns. Make three copies of the Triceratops patterns on page 83—each on a different color of construction paper. Laminate and then cut out the patterns. Use a hole puncher to make a hole at the top of each cutout. Thread a length of yarn through the hole in each cutout; then tie the yarn ends together to make a Triceratops necklace. Place three large plastic hoops on the floor. Give each of nine student volunteers a necklace to wear. Explain that the students will perform a dance—The Triceratops Tromp— while some lively music is being played. Stop the music periodically and call out either the word, "Color," or "Size." Have the children check their necklaces for that attribute, then sort themselves into the plastic hoops accordingly. (For instance, when the word "Color" is called, the students wearing identically colored necklaces will assemble in one hoop. In similar fashion, students wearing Triceratops necklaces of the same size will gather in one hoop when the word "Size" is called.) When the students have sorted themselves by the given attribute, each hoop will be occupied by three students. After the first round of play, invite nine different volunteers to wear the necklaces and participate in the activity. Continue in similar fashion until every child has had the opportunity to play.

Fast Food

After learning of tiny Compsognathus's speedy movements, students will have a new definition for fast food—and will enjoy capturing some for their own snacks! Prior to this activity, tie a length of yarn to a spring-type clothespin; then prepare a zippered plastic bag of dinosaur-shaped fruit snacks for each child. Explain that Compsognathus used its sharp eyes to search for lizards and insects. When prey was spotted, this chicken-sized dinosaur would quickly run to capture its meal.

Divide your class into student pairs. Have one student clip the clothespin to a bag of snacks and use the yarn to slowly drag the bag along a grassy area so that it resembles an animal's or insect's movements. Ask his partner to position himself a distance from the first child and to role-play a Compsognathus in search of food. As soon as he spots his prey, encourage the Compsognathus to run as fast as possible to capture it. After he captures his food, have the child remove the clothespin from the bag; then invite the partners to exchange roles so that each has the opportunity to role-play the dinosaur. If desired, time each student's run with a stopwatch; then write his time on a notecard. Encourage the students to identify the written numeral. After every student has captured his snack, invite the class to leisurely enjoy their fast food.

With Respect To The King

Youngsters will be roaring with laughter by the time they finish singing this reverent—but silly—song that may well express how the other dinosaurs felt toward Tyrannosaurus rex, the "tyrant-lizard king." Inform youngsters that Tyrannosaurus rex was perhaps the most intimidating dinosaur of all time with his large head, sharp claws, and fiercely sharp teeth. Display a picture of Tyrannosaurus rex from *The Big Book Of Dinosaurs: A First Book For Young Children* by Angela Wilkes (Dorling Kindersley Publishing, Inc.) or any other illustrated picture source; then teach little ones this song and the accompanying gestures. Have youngsters repeat the song three times, increasing the tempo of the tune for each repetition. Conclude the last verse with an emphatic "Please!"

Unique Dinosaurs

Imaginations will soar as each youngster creates her own dinosaur mask, headband, or cap in this activity. Stock your art center with a supply of paper plates, sentence strips, and inexpensive painter's caps. Provide a variety of craft items, such as fabric paint, sheets of craft foam, assorted colors and textures of paper, wiggle eyes, packing peanuts, yarn, and lots of glue. Invite each child to use the materials to make her choice of a mask, headband, or cap to resemble a dinosaur. After the projects are completed, snap a photograph of each child wearing her creation. Attach a notecard labeled with the child's dictated name for her dinosaur to the bottom of each photograph. Display the photos with sentence strips labeled with the rhyme " 'Me-a-saurs.' 'You-a-saurs.' We Are All 'Unique-a-saurs'! "

Tyrannosaurus Rex, My Dear
(sung to the tune
of "John Jacob Jingleheimer Schmidt")

Tyrannosaurus rex, my dear,
Show "claws"; then fold hands across chest.
You cause such fear!
Frightened look on face.
When your sharp teeth you show,
Point to bared teeth.
I know it's time to go!
Quickly flutter hands away from body.
Tyrannosaurus rex, my dear,
Show "claws"; then fold hands across chest.
Da-da-da-da-don't eat me!
Shake finger in front of body.
(Last verse only) PLEASE!
Fold hands together in front as if to beg.

Trey-a-saur

80

I would live in a skyscraper.

If I Were A Dinosaur

Involve youngsters in an imaginary modern-day adventure filled with dinosaur doings. In advance duplicate and cut apart the booklet cover and pages on pages 84–85 for each child. Then read aloud *If The Dinosaurs Came Back* by Bernard Most (Harcourt Brace & Company). Invite students to discuss the story's suggestions on how dinosaurs could be useful if they lived today. Do the students think that the book depicts the way it would really be? Then invite each child to stretch his imagination a little further by imagining himself as a modern-day dinosaur. Have him illustrate each page of his booklet and dictate a completion to each corresponding sentence. Ask him to color the picture on the cover and write his name on the blank line. Sequence the completed cover and pages, and staple them together along the left side. Encourage student partners to read their booklets to each other.

Fact And Fiction About Our Fossilized Friends

Danny And The Dinosaur
Written by Syd Hoff
Published by Scholastic Inc.

The Dinosaur Who Lived In My Backyard
Written by B. G. Hennessy
Published by Puffin Books

Can I Have A Stegosaurus, Mom? Can I? Please!?
Written by Lois G. Grambling
Published by BridgeWater Books

Dinosaurs, Dinosaurs
Written by Byron Barton
Published by Thomas Y. Crowell

Dinosaurs
Written by Gail Gibbons
Published by Scholastic Inc.

Time Flies
Written by Eric Rohmann
Published by Scholastic Inc.

Dinosaur Roar!
Written by Paul and Henrietta Stickland
Published by Dutton Children's Books

Bones, Bones, Dinosaur Bones
Written by Byron Barton
Published by Thomas Y. Crowell

Count-A-Saurus
Written by Nancy Blumenthal
Published by Scholastic Inc.

Dinosaur Skeletons Flannelboard Figures
Use with "Bony Connections" on page 77.

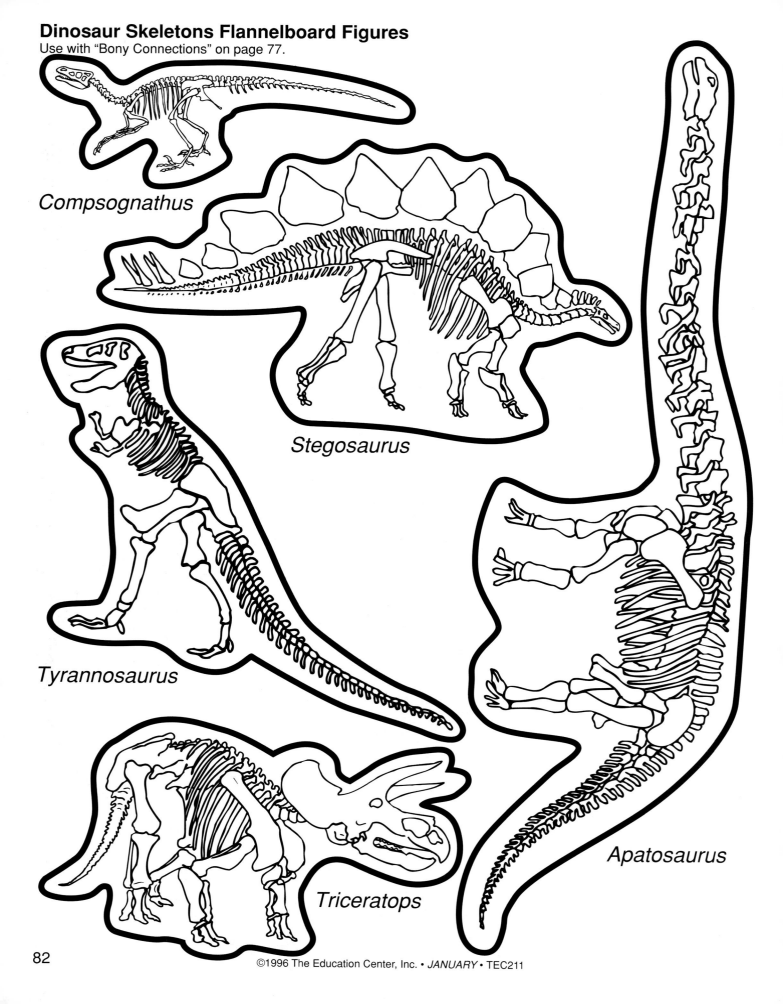

Compsognathus

Stegosaurus

Tyrannosaurus

Triceratops

Apatosaurus

1

I would be a

_____.

If I Were
A Dinosaur...

by _____

84

3

I would help _____.

2

I would live _____.

Calling All Community Helpers!

Invite youngsters to learn all about the workers who serve their communities with this unit focusing on real experiences and dramatic play.

ideas contributed by Ada Hanley Goren and Ann Saunders

Classroom Careers

Chances are that you routinely assign classroom jobs to your students. Help youngsters make the connection between their responsibilities in the classroom and jobs performed by workers in the real world. As you talk about the responsibilities associated with each of your classroom jobs, ask youngsters if they can think of a real job that is similar. Then announce new job titles and show youngsters the equipment they'll be using to perform each job. Take some suggestions from the list below or make up some of your own.

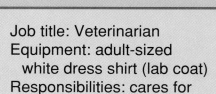

Meteorologist
Caroline Hodnett

Job title: Veterinarian
Equipment: adult-sized white dress shirt (lab coat)
Responsibilities: cares for class pets

Job title: Farmer
Equipment: gardening gloves
Responsibilities: cares for classroom plants

Job title: Tour Guide
Equipment: special visor
Responsibilities: leads the class to each destination outside the classroom (line leader)

Job title: Mail Carrier
Equipment: canvas tote bag
Responsibilities: passes out papers and supplies

Job title: Waitperson
Equipment: tray
Responsibilities: helps to serve snacks and meals

Job title: Secretary
Equipment: special pencil
Responsibilities: helps take attendance and lunch count

Now that you've revamped your classroom jobs, use the cards on pages 93 and 95 to create a new job board. First duplicate pages 94 and 96 for later use. Then mount pages 93 and 95 on sheets of tagboard. Cut the cards apart; then laminate all the cards for durability and repeated programming. Program the blank cards with jobs specific to your classroom. Each time you make new job assignments, print a child's name on each card with a wipe-off marker. Post the cards on a bulletin board or in a pocket chart with the title "We're On The Job!"

Live And In Person

Enhance your youngsters' study of community helpers' jobs by arranging field trips or classroom visits from workers. Consider planning a trip to a local police station, hospital, fire station, or post office during this unit. You may also want to plan visits from some of the workers whose careers you'll be discussing. Ask them to bring along any equipment, uniforms, or other visual aids that will help explain their jobs to your little ones. Ask some parents of your youngsters to speak about their jobs or to donate props and costumes for use in discussions and dramatic play.

The Play's The Thing

Your youngsters will benefit from role-playing community helpers' jobs. Transform your dramatic-play area to resemble a community helper's work setting. Use the suggestions below to get started or create a unique center of your own!

Post Office: Arrange furniture to resemble a counter. Add props such as stickers, rubber stamps, stamp pads, paper, envelopes, writing utensils, old junk mail, small scales, boxes, canvas tote bags, a toy cash register, and play money. Create a mailbox from a cardboard box. Provide short-sleeved men's dress shirts to serve as uniforms. Now you're ready for some first-class fun!

Veterinarian's Office: Arrange furniture to simulate a waiting room and an examination room. In the waiting room, provide a toy telephone, magazines, and books. In the exam room, mount posters of domestic animals on the wall and add props such as a toy doctor's bag with medical tools, bandages, cotton balls, empty medicine bottles, notepads, and pencils. Add a supply of stuffed animals to serve as patients. The doctor will see you now!

Store: Add some bookshelves to the area and arrange other furniture to resemble a counter. As a group, decide what type of merchandise you'd like to sell; then ask for donations from parents to stock your classroom store. (Items like fake jewelry, silk and plastic flowers, or inexpensive toys—such as those from fast-food restaurant meals—are good possibilities.) Arrange the merchandise on the shelves; then add props such as a toy cash register or calculator, play money, a toy telephone, notepads, pencils, price tags, and bags. Your store is open for business!

Restaurant: Arrange furniture to simulate a dining area and a kitchen area. Provide props such as paper menus, dishes, utensils, plastic food, aprons, pots and pans, notepads, pencils, a toy cash register and play money, a toy telephone, pitchers, and trays. Containers of play dough will serve as the ingredients for some tasty meals!

What Is My Job?

Teach youngsters this repetitive song about the various jobs in your community. At the end of each verse, ask children to raise their hands if they can guess what worker does the job described in that verse. For example, a volunteer might respond that the first verse describes a doctor, a nurse, or any health-care worker.

(sung to the tune of "Are You Sleeping?")

What is my job?
What is my job?
Can you guess?
Can you guess?
[I help people get well.]
[I help people get well.]
Who am I?
Who am I?

Repeat the verse as many times as desired, replacing the underlined phrase with a phrase from the list below (or make up one of your own).

I can fix the water pipes. (plumber)
I deliver letters. (mail carrier)
I make tasty meals for you. (cook, parent)
I keep your pets healthy. (veterinarian)
I can teach you new things. (teacher)
I can help if you get lost. (police officer)

Read All About Them!

It won't be hard work to get youngsters interested in community helpers when you share these wonderful selections!

Busy People
Written by Nick Butterworth
Published by Candlewick Press

Martin's Hats
Written by Joan W. Blos
Published by William Morrow And Company

Whose Hat?
Written by Margaret Miller
Published by Greenwillow Books

Who Uses This?
Written by Margaret Miller
Published by Scholastic Inc.

Community Helpers Up Close

After providing an overview of many different community helpers, focus students' attention on some individual jobs in the workforce.

Police Officer

If you haven't invited a police officer to speak to your class, discuss this important job. Emphasize the police officer's role in promoting the *safety* of citizens. Then invite youngsters to role-play an interaction with a police officer. Have one student pretend to be lost, and have another child (equipped with a pad and pencil) play the part of a helpful police officer. Encourage the lost child to give important personal information to help the officer locate his parents. Ask younger children to give their full names. Older children may be able to recite their addresses or phone numbers. Have the police officer "write" this information on his pad, then pretend to use it to help the child find his family.

After every child has had a turn to role-play an officer or a lost child, conclude your activity by awarding each youngster an honorary treat—an edible police badge! Roll out refrigerated sugar-cookie dough on a floured surface; then have each child use a star-shaped cookie cutter to cut out a cookie badge. Then give him some dough scraps and ask him to roll five small balls of dough. Have him press one ball of dough onto each point of his star. Bake the cookies as directed on the package. Cool the cookies; then invite each child to frost his cookie with white icing. Have him place a silver, ball-shaped cake decoration on each of his cookie's rounded points. Then encourage your youngsters to bite into those badges!

Firefighter

Many youngsters are fascinated with the job of a firefighter. Share the pictures from a photo-illustrated book about firefighters on the job—such as *Fire Fighters* by Robert Maass (Scholastic Inc.)—to stimulate a discussion about this important job. Then follow up your discussion with this red-hot art project! Invite each youngster to draw a picture of a house on a sheet of paper. Encourage each child to glue torn pieces of red, orange, and yellow construction paper onto her house picture to represent the flames of a fire. After the glue has dried, invite students to role-play the job of firefighters. Place a protective covering over the paint tray of an easel and on the floor below the easel. Working with one child at a time, attach her picture to the easel. If desired, provide a child-sized raincoat, rubber boots, and firefighter's helmet for the child to wear. Give her a spray bottle filled with a mixture of white tempera paint and water. Explain that the bottle represents a fire extinguisher and her job is to "put out the fire" on her paper. While she "extinguishes" the house fire, have her classmates imitate the sound of a fire engine's siren. Then give the next child a turn to spray away!

Charles

Doctor

Learning about health-care professionals will be in the bag with this activity! Begin by sharing the photo-illustrated book *When I See My Doctor…* by Susan Kuklin (Bradbury Press) to stimulate a discussion about the jobs of doctors and nurses. Invite your students to share their experiences about visits to the doctor's office. Then take a closer look at the tools that are used by health-care workers. If possible, show the children some real medical equipment borrowed from a parent or a local medical office. Then invite each child to create his own doctor's bag.

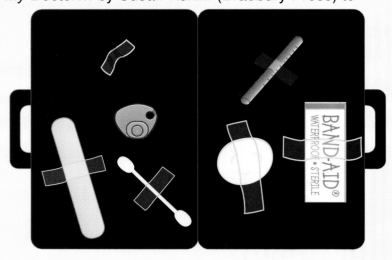

For each child, fold and cut a 12" x 18" sheet of black construction paper as shown. Have each child glue a red, construction-paper cross to the outside of his bag. Use a white crayon to write "Dr. [child's name]" above the cross. Then provide each of your diminutive doctors with some tools to store in his bag.

Create pretend thermometers by cutting clear plastic straws into halves; then use a permanent black marker to make lines on one side of each straw half. Provide each child with a pretend stethoscope—a length of yarn threaded through two holes punched in opposite sides of an egg-carton cup and tied into a necklace. Have each child open (unfold) his doctor's bag and tape his thermometer and stethoscope—as well as a cotton ball, an adhesive bandage, a tongue depressor, and a cotton swab—to the inside of his bag. Invite each child to take his bag home to share with his family.

Carpenter

Switch youngsters' attention to another type of tools—those used by a carpenter. Share the book *A Carpenter* by Douglas Florian (Greenwillow Books) for a simple look at the job

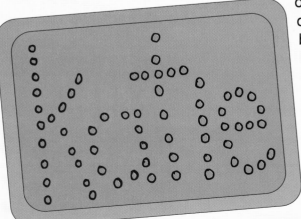

of a carpenter and the tools he uses. Display some of the tools shown in the book. Ask youngsters to brainstorm some ways to use the tools safely. Show them a pair of safety goggles and ask if anyone knows what they are used for. Then invite youngsters to make their own imitation safety goggles. Provide each child with two pipe cleaners and a set of two rings cut from a six-pack beverage holder. Demonstrate how to twist a pipe cleaner around the outer edge of each plastic ring to form a pair of goggles. Help each student bend the pipe cleaners to fit around her ears.

Now that the children have safety goggles to wear, it's tool time! Invite small groups of youngsters to don their goggles and use plastic hammers to pound golf tees into Styrofoam® meat trays. Encourage youngsters to hammer designs, shapes, letters, numbers, or their names into their trays. Carpet squares placed beneath the trays will muffle the pounding, but not the fun!

Storekeeper

Your youngsters have probably visited many different kinds of stores. Ask them to brainstorm a list of as many kinds of stores as they can think of for you to write on the chalkboard or a sheet of chart paper. Then read the story *On Market Street* by Arnold Lobel (Scholastic Inc.) for a mention of even more merchandise! Ask your students to decide what types of merchandise they'd like to sell if they were storekeepers.

Duplicate the class-book page on page 94 for each child. On his page, have each student draw pictures or glue cut-out pictures of items he'd like to sell in his store. Write his dictation on the blank line. Use two 12" x 18" sheets of construction paper to create front and back covers for the book. Stack the pages together; then center the stack along the bottom long edge of one of the sheets of construction paper. Staple the stack in place along the top edge of the pages. Position the other sheet of construction paper on top of the first, aligning and stapling together each side edge and the top edge. Cut the top sheet of construction paper to fold open as shown; then draw handles on the resulting doors. Print the title "Our Store Story" across the top of the cover. Read the finished book to your youngsters, and then place it in your classroom library for further enjoyment by your young entrepreneurs!

Truck Driver

How do all those shoes, toys, flowers, and groceries get to the stores where they're sold? In trucks, of course! Teach youngsters more about trucks and truck drivers when you show the video *Close Up And Very Personal: Big Rigs* (available from Stage Fright Productions, 1-800-979-6800). After viewing the video, engage your youngsters in towing some goods cross-classroom with this fun math activity.

To prepare, place several toy dump trucks or trailer trucks in your block area. Place an equal number of boxes or baskets on the other side of the classroom. On the side of each truck, tape a slip of paper with a numeral printed on it. On the side of each box or basket, tape a slip of paper with a numeral that corresponds to one shown on one of the trucks.

Then invite a few children to each choose a truck to "drive." Instruct each child to identify the number on his truck. Then have him place that number of blocks (or other small manipulatives, depending on the size of your toy trucks) in his truck. Each student may then "drive" his truck across the room to its destination—the box or basket with the corresponding number. Once there, have the drivers unload their cargo. Have them count the blocks to make sure they're delivering the whole order! Then have those drivers make a return trip to the block area so a new set of truck drivers can make their deliveries!

What Does Your Mommy Do?

Get parents involved in your study of community helpers with this picture-perfect activity. Begin by reading the books *Mommies At Work* and *Daddies At Work,* both by Eve Merriam (published by Simon & Schuster Children's Books). After sharing the books, ask each youngster to describe what his mommy and/or daddy do for a living. Then duplicate the parent note on page 96 to get parents involved in a classroom keepsake about their jobs.

Have each student take home a copy of the note on page 96 for each of his parents to complete. As each child returns his notes, read the parental descriptions and share the photos with your class. Then add each note to a three-ring binder. Make a construction-paper cover for the binder which reads "Mommies And Daddies At Work." Youngsters will enjoy looking through the binder again and again, and it will help them realize that Mommy and Daddy are hard at work while they're away at school!

Dear Family:
As part of our study of community helpers, we are putting together a class book about our mommies' and daddies' jobs. Please take a moment to describe your job (even if you work in the home). Then—if possible—attach a photo of yourself in your workplace. We appreciate your efforts!

My name is _____Miriam Mayhew_____.

I am a(n) _____kindergarten teacher_____.

I work at _____Sommerdale Primary_____.

Some of the things I do every day include:

reading stories, singing with the kids

sharing knowledge, cooking

creating art,

helping , and

The thing I like best about my job is

working with young children.

This is a picture of me at work.

Frankie

I want to be a scenic designer when I grow up so I can paint big stuff in a theatre.

When I Grow Up...

Conclude your community helpers unit by posing the often-asked question, "What do you want to be when you grow up?" Then create a bulletin-board display to show off your youngsters' replies! Ready an instant camera and gather together a variety of props and costumes used throughout your unit (such as the ones described in "Classroom Careers" on page 86 and "The Play's The Thing" on page 87). Ask each child to tell what he wants to be when he grows up and give a reason why. Write his dictation on the bottom of a sheet of construction paper. Then invite him to choose from among the costumes or hold a prop appropriate to that job. Snap his photo and invite him to watch the picture develop. Then glue it above his dictation on his sheet of paper. Display all the papers on a bulletin board with the title "When We Grow Up—As You Will See—This Is What We Want To Be!"

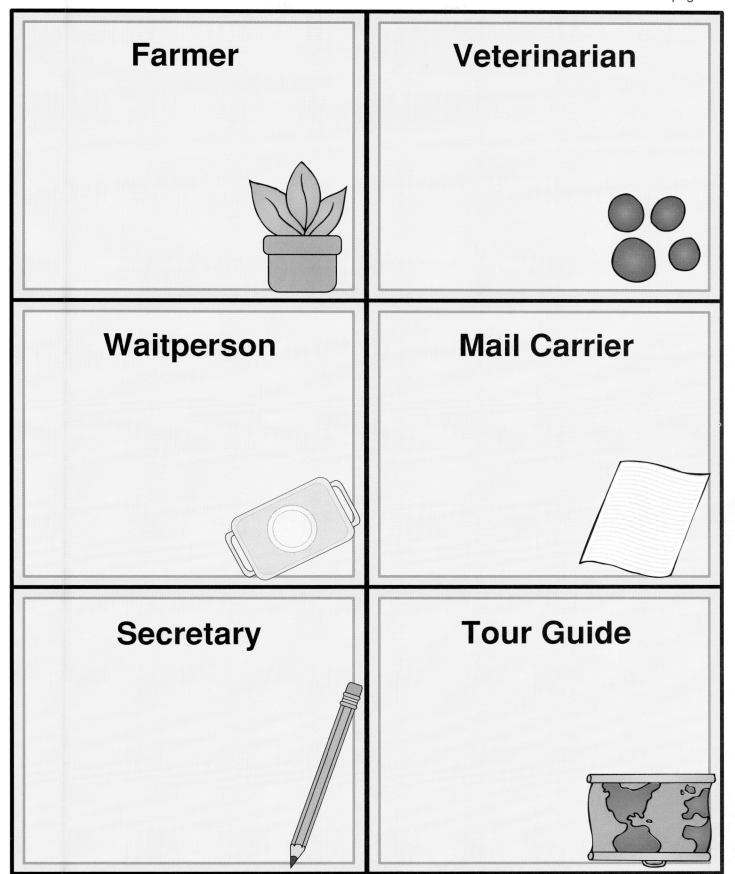

Farmer

Veterinarian

Waitperson

Mail Carrier

Secretary

Tour Guide

If I had a store, I would sell _____.

Note To The Teacher: Use this page with "Storekeeper" on page 91.

94

Librarian

Custodian

Meteorologist

Dear Family:
   As part of our study of community helpers, we are putting together a class book about our mommies' and daddies' jobs. Please take a moment to describe your job (even if you work in the home). Then—if possible—attach a photo of yourself in your workplace.
   We appreciate your efforts!

My name is _____.

I am a(n) _____.

I work at _____.

Some of the things I do every day include:

_____,

_____,

_____, and

_____.

The thing I like best about my job is _____.

This is a picture
of me at work.

©1996 The Education Center, Inc. • *JANUARY* • TEC211

96   **Note To The Teacher:** Use with "What Does Your Mommy Do?" on page 92.